f u l l a l o v e

Also by Gordon Burn

Fiction
Alma Cogan

Non-fiction
Somebody's Husband, Somebody's Son:
The Story of the Yorkshire Ripper

Pocket Money: Bad Boys, Business Heads
and Boom-time Snooker

f u l l a l o v e

Gordon Burn

Secker & Warburg
London

From *Molloy* by Samuel Beckett, translated by Samuel Beckett in association with Patrick Bowles, reprinted by kind permission of The Samuel Beckett Estate and The Calder Education Trust, London.

From 'Marito in Citta', © 1978 by John Cheever, reprinted by kind permission of Alfred A. Knopf, Inc.

'Detroit City', written by Danny Dill and Mel Tillis, © 1963 Polygram Music Publishing Ltd, lyrics reproduced by kind permission of the publisher.

Lyric reproduction of 'Is it My Body' by kind permission of Carlin Music Corp., UK administrator.

From *World Within World*, © 1951 by Stephen Spender, reprinted by kind permission of the author.

The author wishes to acknowledge his debt to
the work, particularly the doll works,
of the American artist Mike Kelley.

First published in Great Britain in 1995
by Martin Secker & Warburg Limited,
an imprint of Reed Consumer Books Limited,
Michelin House, 81 Fulham Road, London SW3 6RB
and Auckland, Melbourne, Singapore and Toronto

A CIP catalogue record for this book
is available from the British Library
ISBN 0 436 20059 7

Phototypeset by Intype, London
Printed and bound in Great Britain
by Mackays of Chatham plc,
Chatham, Kent

To Carol Gorner

Until the day when, your endurance gone,
in this world for you without arms,
you catch up in yours the first mangy cur you meet,
carry it the time needed for it to love you
and you it, then throw it away

Samuel Beckett, *Molloy*

O : N : E

As a hack, a scribbler, a fully benefited and BUPA-ed pen performer (note the absence of ironising inverted commas: I use the language of self-loathing that characterises this wall-shinning, nose-poking, leg-in-the-door end of the trade knowingly and deliberately, without any ironic intent), it has to occur to me whether I am an actual carrier, a cross-pollinator of misery and annihilating despair and doorstep human anguish, and not merely its privileged witness. There it is, and, quick as you can say 'The coffin was so tiny that it took your breath away', there I am — breast-pocket tape recorder freshly batteried, notebook fatted with quotes for dead stories, cancelled with strokes of wristy finality; biro primed. Although I couldn't claim it was the way I saw the last working years of my life turning out, I seem to have become, all against expectation and any natural inclination, the miseried's, the disastered's, the lifelorn's, the victims' (most of all the victims'), friend.

Copy filed with an implied catch in the voice, a muffled sob in the throat, sentimental as a lollypop. A terrible command of the fine gradations in the purple spectrum, from lavender mist to damson dipso blush. These are my apparent strengths. You might have read my stuff. It might even be your turn to talk to me, tragic mum, grief-stricken dad, when the runaway pantechnicon crashes your tidy terrace or City's south stand collapses or the police are on the trail of the next evil sex fiend. (Think of it: the poignant details of your life, your plain statements coleslawed into something weightless, sizeless, and travelling at the speed of light within information networks depending not on dirty wheels, gears, pistons, rivets or hot engines, but on minute components, invisible processes, intangible – incomprehensible – technologies.)

One certain thing. Life keeps coming. It keeps coming and coming. Celebrities, money, babies, violence, messy death . . . What else? Animals. Sex. Perm two from seven for a result; perm three from seven for a real marmalade dropper. The news as a production line with no beginning and no end. Life in the perpetual present. Nothing's new. Not a lot is new. Things that happened two days ago – things I witnessed first-hand, that I reported on; the town I visited, the stunts I connived in setting up, the quotes that filled my book – are already foggy for me.

I feel a kind of numbness in my short-term memory, although I have long regarded this as my natural condition and probably a condition for going into this line of work. When I grew up as a boy in the north of England, there wasn't much, so when I arrived in London I had nothing, and I forgot what little I had up there. The hospital where I was born is now the Happy Dragon Chinese restaurant. The school that I attended is now a discount mall developed by a boy who went to school there with me, one of the great local boom-boom 1980s success stories. (We ran a picture of him in a recent business section, as it happens: he was posed sweatily with a group of shelf-stackers and perox-ided checkout girls in a chilled storeroom area: 'A boss is like a diaper – always on your ass and usually full of shit,' a 'novelty' poster said, tacked to a fridge slightly to the left of where the photographer had placed him.) Nodes, the undertakers from where I buried both my parents, is now a branch of Perfect Pizza. I am in the present, I came from nowhere, I can't go back.

You probably think from what you've heard already that you certainly wouldn't talk to me. Well, would you talk to me? Would you tell me your private thoughts and memories, spill your guts? Would you vouchsafe me your keepsakes and mementoes – the ethereally lit studio portrait that leaves a pale space where it was hanging, a light line in the dust where it was standing; the vignetted picture from your wallet? Would you trust me with the home video of the last time you were all together – X removing something from the oven, X red-faced, giggling, shaking a curtain of hair in front of her pretty face to shield it from the camera – before the bombers struck, before the stranger lurched from the shadows? Of course you would. I'm not wrong. Believe me. As I say, this is my area of operation; my specialised subject; my purlieu; my arena. Beats writing about chocolate bunnies at Easter, I always say. I always say (and when I say it there *is* some irony intended, although it is an irony I fancy is lost on the editor and his near-identically-dressed team of executive brown-nosers, ever alert for new targets of opportunity) – looking them straight in the tie, I always say: Wind me up, chief, and point me at it.

We're a tabloid outfit, positioned in the middle-market, some distance upwind of the cro-magnon Fun-Puzzlers and lip-movers. But – although this was truer in the past than it has become recently – I'm not a leg man. A dawn raider. Bish-bash-bosh. Who, what, when and where. What 'Tosser'

3

Dosson, my editor, a Streeter of the old school, likes to call the 'geography' of a story. I'm a colour man. That is: I colour it up; give it a bit of ginger. I help keep the heat under a story by providing a tarty next-day take on what everybody already knows.

I go in with the second-wave. Which these days means that my days are dogged by flowers. My path is strewn with them. Flowers mark the spot.

The flowers come wrapped in all the surfaces of cheap living – klaxon colours, slippery prophylactic textures. As soon as the tape markers are removed, women begin steering children forward clutching thin, apologetic bunches of pinks and gyp and grade-two tulips in flattened cones that imitate laminated woodgrain and fake marble, beaten copper and satin-aluminium fire surrounds, duvet- and ironingboard-covers, silver-frosted ceiling sconces, the technologised waffle-treads of trainers, glancing football shirt shadow-patterns, blistery thermoplastics, the foam-backed leather-like finish of wedding albums.

The effect aimed for in the impromptu pavement shrines marking the site of the latest nail-bomb or child-snatch or brutal sex-death is peaceful, pastoral, consolatory – the evocation of some dappled bluebell wood or country church-yard or Dairylea buttercup meadow, a world away from the 144-point hurts of the raw modern city.

In reality, though, the flower-heaped memorials are just another variety of urban utterance. In the first hours, the railway embankments, playing-field perimeters, tower-block entrances and shopping-precinct seating islands are transformed as if by flooded lighting or a freak fall of snow. What was concrete and familiar suddenly seems defamiliarised, *derealised*; the backdrop to a dream.

People crowd at the edge of the oddly regular weave of the blankets of flowers, stunned by the scale of what they have made. (I've noticed – but naturally haven't written: it wouldn't get in if I did write it – that an element of civic competitiveness has started creeping in, as if compassion was quantifiable and could be measured in square-footage and drift-thickness and overall depth of cover.)

But soon (very soon when there has been some weather – a bitter north-easterly clawing at the filmy wrappings, scattering them in shop doorways and bus shelters, pasting them round bollards and railings, throwing them to the wind; persistent rain pounding them into a sodden pulp) they turn into just one more example of urban blight; of city sadness. By the time the story has moved down the page or been buried inside the paper, the memorials start to look like flocks of tick-infested pigeons, or the water-logged communal bedding in some cardboard city. The poor colours bleed and fade. The soft toys that have been put there – the Snoopys and velveteen bunnies and bag-eyed Pound Puppies – moult and burst along the seams and spill their no longer loveable or huggable wetted kapok guts.

I know I have squeezed a story until its pips are squeaking when the smell of rotted vegetation starts to lift off the bank or trench of remembrances and the mechanical shovels and power-hoses of the refuse departments start preparing to move in. 'Under the wide and starry sky', 'Love's last gift – remembrance', 'Bitterness serves no purpose and corrodes the soul', 'A little angel lost in flight' is the sort of thing it says on the smashed condolence cards they leave in their wake, and I have built up a small collection of these. A selection of them, bordered in butterflies and blurry mis-keyed flowers and cupids, green-stained, the inks running, was posted round my office computer until a protest got up by one of the squeamier pencil pushers, and including Mahalia, the regular cleaner, who left notes telling me I was a sorryfuck who could empty his own bins, succeeded in having them removed. ' "Life's a shit-sandwich" is what they should say,' I told them in retaliation, in my bloodier moments. ' "Life's a bucket of warm spit." '

My name – my *byline*, when I get one these days – is Norman Miller. It used to be a picture byline in the old days, back in what to me now seems the long, long ago: a reversed-out mug shot over my name done in a distinctive, bulging type, all curves and Mickey ears, that signalled 'soft' features rather than the unrelenting hard-news beat I find myself pounding now.

Norman Miller. Four brick dull, plain artisanal syllables, bequeathed to me by my poor dull parents, but given an unlooked-for metropolitan sheen by their near-duplication of the name of 'the champ of writers', as I once heard the then heavyweight champion, George Foreman, call Mailer, to his beaming delight: he lit up like Christmas, at the same time wiping his feet in a backwards direction on the carpet, as if he had just discovered dogshit on his shoes. (I watched him repeat the performance when I expressed my own – fumbling but genuine – admiration for his work.)

Norman Miller/Norman Mailer. It has been a lucky consonance, and one used consciously and entirely shamelessly by me to get the ear of the subliterate, the disliterate, the pain crazed, the grief engulfed, the halt, and the lazy of hearing. 'Norman Miller'. Crooned in that face-in-the-phone creepy-confidential manner perfected, when in pursuit of a story, by all the members of my profession.

6

The disappointment on the faces of taxi drivers, hotel managers, PR representatives, fast-fodder interviewees and others when they come face to face not with the celebrity scribe, suited by Jones, Chalk and Dawson of Sackville Street, shod by John Lobb of St James's (a lasting legacy of his marriage to Lady Jeanne, daughter of the Duke of Argyll), twinkly and burly and with a head of hair, though snowy white, still testosterone-rich in early old age, coming forward with his chipper old bandy-legged sailor walk – 'Gangway for all this talent!' . . . their sense of let-down, of being on the end of some mild confidence trickery when confronted not by Mailer but by Miller, who, for all his presentability and plausibility bears the unmistakable, authentic whiff of Fleet Street (five parts Stolly to three parts Youngs Special bitter to two parts YSL 'Jazz', plus an aura of something that comics call 'flop sweat', something they give off when they're dying on their feet – hear me: I'm dying on my feet) – this sense of let-down is something I long ago accepted as a saddening but not all-undermining fact of life.

My path and Mailer's have crossed, as you will by now have gathered; but they have crossed only once. This I think was in – if I had a cuttings book, a graveyard of my deathless, which I haven't, I could look it up – 1974. I would be thirty-two then and, after a number of years spent hosing vomit off other people's copy, just starting to rise above the grind as a writer. (I was also only four years away from personal meltdown in 1974, from the 'spiritual emergency' (thank you, doctor) that's put me here, spinning my wheels, dosed up the wazoo, but of course I couldn't know that then.)

By the time *he* was thirty-two, Mailer already had three novels (and two wives) (and a spell in Bellevue, the local cuckoo-nest, the result of skewering wife number two with a Swiss Army knife) under his belt, and, after Hemingway, was probably the most instantly recognisable writer in the world.

As might be expected, I have taken a keener-than-usual interest in Mailer's career. It was his side-step into journalism – a kind of journalism – towards the end of the sixties that gave me part of the push that I needed to give up my haemorrhoid-hatching inside job to see what it was like knocking stories together 'in the field' – meaning, on car bonnets, in piss-stinking telephone booths, and in roaring hostile cafés and bars. Not, I realised, that this was Mailer's chosen MO. And, if I hadn't realised, he patiently spelled it out to me one night after a steady intake of gin rickeys under a reed-thatch umbrella at the outside bar of the Interconti-nental hotel in what had once been Leopoldville in the Belgian Congo but which, by that time, was Kinshasa, in Zaire. We were there to see if Muhammad Ali could regain the heavyweight championship by beating George Foreman, in a Don King–President Mobutu promotion.

'Reporters,' Mailer said, shoulders rolling in an old pug manner even while seated, 'have the middle-class penchant' (he pronounced this the American way, stressing the 'e', sounding the 't') 'for collecting tales, stories, legends, accounts of practical jokes, details of negotiation, bits of memoir. There is nobody more practical than a reporter. He exhibits the same avidity for news which a businessman will show for money.' His eyebrows made a triangle with the line of his eyes, and he barrelled in with his fists on his knees, as he tends to do when he's got off one good line and already has a topper coming. 'No bourgeois will hesitate to pick up a dollar, even if he is not fond of the man with whom he is dealing. So, a reporter will do a nice story about a type he dislikes, or a bad story about a figure he is fond of. I always had some dim intuitive feeling that what was wrong with all journalism was that the reporter tended to be objective and that that was one of the great lies of all time. Now it is more *comfortable* to write that way . . .' I didn't know if I was being personally got at, but that's how I felt. I felt the rims of my ears hurting red in the cooling night. But it had already become difficult to converse by then because of the nightly, eleven-on-the-button 'Soirée Africaine': seven topless, melon-breasted girls dancing to the sound of drums in La Cascade, the garden restaurant beside the swimming pool. Three of them were performing to loud rhythmic applause with glasses of beer balanced impassively on their heads.

Good material, I suggested to Mailer, who in ten days I hadn't seen take a note. 'Material?' he said, evacuating a Santa-size ho-ho. 'Tell you. I wouldn't recognise material these days if it smacked me in the mouth.'

I didn't know spit about boxing. But then, knowing nothing about painting hadn't stopped me banging out 1500 words on the references to Indian totems, Graeco-Roman legends and animal sexuality in the early works of Jackson Pollock, any more than being innumerate had inhibited me from banging a piece together on Tunku Abdul Rahman's financial restructuring of the Malaysian economy. The first article I wrote for my first London paper was an obituary of the American dancer Ruth St Denis, whose name I read for the first time when the file folder containing her taped-together, ash-like clippings dropped on my desk.

I kept hearing names in Kinshasa, and having people – mainly waddy, vending-machine-sized black men with broken boot heels and deep scratches on their wraparound glasses – pointed out to me excitedly across plastic palatial rooms frantic with electrostatic that did unpredictable things to all the hairpieces present. Barney Ross, Willie Pep, Ezzard Charles, Benny Paret . . . Who were these people? Bob Clemo, the paper's star boxing writer, could have told me. But, for complicated domestic reasons – was this the time his wife hurled herself into the canal near where they lived in Maida Vale wearing only a poncho and self-suspend stockings? Or the time their son, radged that his ounce of Lebanese red had disappeared from the toe of a pair of school sneakers, arsoned the same house? Or maybe Clemo had simply been shipped off to Champneys again for drying out on the paper's account? – whatever the reason, Bob Clemo wasn't flying in until forty-eight hours before fight-time.

When he finally did, within a few hours of deplaning he was circling the dining-table like a paso-doble dancer without a partner, in preparation for his world-renowned whip-the-cloth-off act. (He insisted that all the plates and bottles and everything were *supposed* to end up in a dribbling, pooling heap in the middle. He earned a cheer anyway for giving his expenses such a heroic first hiding.) By 4 a.m., Clemo and his opposite number on one of the American papers were battling it out with chairs in the bar – one chair each, wielded at head-height and crashed around until only a couple of staves were remaining, the two of them coming at each other, red dirt and matchwood and glass shards clinging to their clothes, while the Zairois bar boys speculated (I wouldn't be surprised) on the weird possession cults and crazy customs of this roving white tribe.

I should probably say here that all this was in the days when I was working for a 'quality' broadsheet paper; in the days, that is, before I was bumped onto the company's breezier, 'faster format' tabloid title (where I still am), and in a time when even the man from Del Monte would have been able to tell the two apart. The paper which employed me hadn't yet gone to colour – still had men working for it, in fact, who would shake their head sadly over the introduction of pictures onto the front page (and who's to say they weren't right?). The news editor was a man who insisted that his male reporters wear suits and that the few hackettes turn up for work in below-the-knee-length skirts and blouses that, as he euphemised it, colouring to purple, they might wear to a funeral without having to change.

This is all by way of explaining their reactions to the material I started to send back from Zaire.

I had travelled to Africa prepared. Ancestor reverence, secular dance, religious masquerade, rules governing the legal status of strangers, spirit mediumship and spirit possession. I had mugged up on all this. Kinshasa was going to be my shining hour. I had a smart new bush jacket from Abercrombie and Fitch. Oh I was keen. I got even more of an edge when I read in an interview with Mailer on the plane going over that he regarded Africa as being Hemingway's territory (I was carrying a copy of *Green Hills of Africa* in my luggage), and so intended to be particularly on his mettle. That was it then: I was going to go *mano a mano* with my namesake, my nemesis, with my 'sharer' self – an idea that was crazy-arsed then, pathological now. I was going to stop him hoovering up the material and making it his own.

And it wasn't just Mailer. Hunter Thompson, George Plimpton, Bud Schulberg, James Baldwin and dozens of other big-foot reporters were all rattling round Zaire. The thing was (I bleated whenever the office got me on the phone), they had access, something I didn't have; they got to go to the places I couldn't go: the Ali bungalow in the Mobutu compound in N'Sele, just for instance, batting the breeze with Ali's man Bundini, and the trainer, Angelo Dundee – 'Hey, Angie,' they'd call across the marbled spaces of the Intercontinental, lying back largely, 'my man Angie!' (what, we wallflowers were constantly asking each other, were these guys *on*?) – and ride on Ali's bus and in the limos and sit on the counterpane in the bedroom at the house while Ali brought himself a Coke from the dresser, his *toto* playing taps on his great ebony trunk of a tufted thigh . . . Not to mention the breakfasts with Mobutu at Mobutu's place by the brown silent river . . .

The result was that I over-reacted. I over-reached. I pushed the envelope. (Where does that come from? What does it mean?) Certainly I over-*wrote*. What they wanted was basic information about Ali's speed or Foreman's bad mood, with a bit of spin here, a bit of vamping-'til-ready there; the tale of the tape. What they got was twenty paragraphs on the ivory market in Kinshasa, the weird house in the centre of town where streams of pygmies constantly came and went, the landscape of the bus ride out to N'Sele (urban shanty, then dusty hot-house exotic), Mobutu's private zoo, Joseph Conrad's Leopoldville contrasted and compared.

But the all-time jaw-dropper was the piece I phoned through on tribal fetish objects, with special reference to the grotesque Zairian nail figure of a two-headed dog which was the first thing I saw when I woke up each morning, and which, on asking round, I discovered wasn't corporate, in the sense of there being one in every room with the pants press, and the hair-drier and the watercolour washes of Mobutu-inspired motorway developments hanging either side of the bed.

I established that these snarling, bristling figures were called *nkisi*, and made particularly excited note of the fact that the 'dried organic matter' clearly visible between some clumps of nails was probably blood from a blood sacrifice, possibly even human blood, possibly even a child's: in certain villages in the interior, a child reported as having disappeared was presumed to have been sacrificed to mark the death of an important local man, and his or her head interred with the chief's body. 'Goodnight, pal,' I would say, made maudlin by the gin rickeys and the Planters Punches and the wine, bearing down on the braille spikes of the dog with a force I now feel sure I hoped would be enough to draw a sample of my own blood, which overnight would trickle down and join up with one of the boluses of ancient encrusted African matter.

I started off with the heel of my hand and then the open palm (violet veined, soft, never exposed to a decent day's toil in its life). Then I brought the *nkisi* in contact with the pad of my bare belly – cold nails hammered in at every angle – my toes enclenched in the flame-retardant carpet – put the two-headed monster on the bed and lay on it, straddled it face-down like a – what? – a fakir? – supported only by extended fingertips and toes, two middle fingers, two big toes, and finally nothing. Kabanga! A jungle moon framed in the high window. A stomach like the take-off board at the triple jump. That new journalism weirdness (although it goes without saying I didn't pass a word of any of this on). Then I'd turn out the light.

My adventures in ethnography went down like the proverbial turd in the punchbowl back in London. The despatches were ruthlessly pruned (as I knew they would be, having been for so long the pruner myself), and pretty soon I fell in with requirements: I rarely left the pack of reporters and filed little that couldn't as easily have been lifted from the morning's press handout or the stuff put over by the Press Association's man. In this way, apart from the necessary topping and tailing, stories virtually wrote themselves.

But until that happened, the blue pencil ran riot on – made Pollocks of – my 'screeds'. ('Made Pollocks of his bollocks' was the joke, neatly combining references to my first and most recent efforts, when I returned home.) I'd get back to the Intercontinental to a stack of message slips all saying the same thing: Contact office soonest. I'd be paged in the lobby and in the coffee-shops and bars, and go to a phone only to have it reiterated that they were not *National Geographic*; that if they'd wanted animal stories they'd have got Johnny Morris, and that, contrary to what I apparently believed, there was no 'a' in my last name (conspiratorial laughter in the background).

The method of paging at the Intercontinental consisted of a bellboy carrying a blackboard sign with Buddhist temple bells tinkling attention to the name of whoever was wanted at the desk or on a phone. 'Martin Bormann', 'Aleister Crowley' and 'Kojak' were popular. And so was 'Norman Mailer'. Or 'Miller'. You could never be sure. Without exception, Mailer's was the name that got chalked up and paraded around. And so invariably, whenever we were both in the hotel, we'd both turn up at the front desk and go through an exaggeratedly formal routine: 'You – No, no, you – No, *please*. You.' Like codgers getting on a train.

' "Norman Miller," ' Mailer said the first time this happened. 'Would I be right in thinking those are Fleet Street eyes? Should I know you?'

' "I really think you are the best journalist in America" –

"Well, Cal, there are days when I think of myself as being the best *writer* in America," ' I said, quoting an exchange that Mailer once had with the poet Robert Lowell. He liked that. It started us off on a good footing. But it wasn't as impromptu as I would like to believe I made it seem. If I'm honest, I suppose I hoped it, or some reference to the Miller/Mailer thing, might sneak into the book-length account of Foreman–Ali that Mailer was in Kinshasa to write. But if I did, I was disappointed – relieved *and* disappointed. A year later, I picked up *The Fight* with the heart-hammering, rib-racketing sense of apprehension anybody feels when they suspect they might be going to see their name in print and have no idea whether they're going to be made to look false or stupid or craven or worse (smaller and greater betrayals, lesser and grosser misrepresentations of which I have been habitually guilty myself in the intervening years). Even vernacular spellings such as 'No'min' and 'Nawmin' came swimming up off the page and made me feel momentarily nauseous.

Somehow – I no longer remember how – among the street jumble of socks, peanuts, toothpaste, chewing-gum, batteries, candles, tins of sardines, cigarettes and used cassette tapes in Kinshasa, I turned up a copy of *An American Dream*, which, on the morning after the fight, both of us still swaying drunk, I got Mailer to sign ('To Norman M. from Norman M. Well met in Kinshasa. Remember (you know this): writers are always selling somebody out. It's been fun.'). It had a supermarket sexy cover, and carried a recommendation from *Time* – 'It races home into the station, blowing all its whistles' – that I have always imagined appearing on a book of mine – a book of course that I have never written, and have now lost all ambition to write.

Yesterday, the twentieth of June, was Father's Day, a fact which went unmarked of course by me, but also by my children (one boy, one girl, both more or less grown up now and effectively moonied by their mother into believing her version of what went wrong in the marriage).

But, as a way, I can only suppose, of flagging its well-known commitment to family-mindedness and 'traditional' family values, this morning's paper has gone overboard with Father's Day mentions. Somebody has run a search and got the computer to spew up a 'topical' add-on for every reference to 'father' or 'daddy' or 'dad.'

So, a man has been gunned down by terrorists in Northern Ireland, 'making a Father's Day widow of his wife, Karen, mother of Susan, 7, and Tony, 8'. One of the England football team has run off with a woman described by his wife as being 'all white shoes and sun-beds', 'leaving sons Michael, 8, and Peter, 7, to spend Father's Day without their dad yesterday, riding their bicycles around the drive of the family's luxury home in Coggeshall, Essex'. A boy of twelve has provided 'the ultimate Father's Day present – the gift of life' by using a tea-towel to staunch the bleeding when a fish tank shattered and sliced through his father's throat and windpipe. I've counted half a dozen references in as many pages.

Even the three paragraphs carrying my puny byline have been given a Father's Day peg. Headlined 'The Look That Says: Live And Let Die, by Norman Miller', they read as follows:

As Scott McGovern continued his fight for life yesterday, the shamed TV star's son was among those attending a star-studded reception at Smith's Lawn, Windsor. Daniel

McGovern, 19, chatted with celebrities including Billy Connolly, Susan Hampshire and Anneka Rice and drank champagne costing £200 a bottle while his father lay on a life support machine in an intensive care unit at St Saviour's Hospital, London. There his condition continued to be described as critical but stable.

It is now 18 days since £750,000-a-year McGovern was found unconscious in his luxury flat at the Barbican. Police are continuing to examine thousands of frames of surveillance footage, including film taken outside the men's toilet on the concourse at Victoria Station, one of the capital's most notorious pick-up places for homosexuals, in an attempt to identify the man spotted entering McGovern's building with him shortly before the murderous attack.

Yesterday McGovern's loyal wife, Sheila, continued her bedside vigil. But Father's Day brought visits from neither of the McGovern children. While Daniel lived it up with the smart set at Windsor, Sophie, 16, was said to be being comforted by family friends.

I wasn't at Smith's Lawn (have never been to Smith's Lawn). I didn't supply the verbals. I didn't read them until I opened this morning's paper. (They were almost certainly lifted from the first edition of the *Express* or the *Mail*.) I'm pretty sure the accompanying picture has been tweaked to bring Dan McGovern into a more intimate relationship with George Michael, whose own image has been electronically realigned – shivered, sphereised – to make him look like somebody suffering from a bad case of the munchies. (This is his most public neurosis, and one therefore that it is always in our interest to tickle up.)

It doesn't matter. Scott McGovern is the big-selling story of the year. 'If it bleeds, it leads.' That's the maxim. So when it's celebrity blood that has been spilled – cowabunga! You're off to the races. Every paper has put on readers since McGovern suffered 'blunt force trauma' – was found with his head stove in by a bronze award statuette based on a maquette by Henry Moore or Barbara Hepworth, one or the other (it's not an aspect of the story we've been climbing over each other to firm up). But cracking copy! Blinding telly! It's been white-knuckle city waiting to see if McGovern comes out of his coma.

Howie Dosson, my editor, doesn't think he will. 'He's seriously kaputted, that guy,' Dosson, generally known as 'Tosser', exulted the minute the news came over the wire. 'Oh are you sure! He is vegetable and will stay vegetable.'

Along with every other human-interest flammer and tabloid footsoldier in the country, I have been on the story since day one. Tosser Dosson made an instant decision to clear the decks. 'You all know what I want,' he said in his Churchillian address, jacketless, two high pulses of colour beating powdery Gainsborough crimson in his cheeks, long metalloid legs astride a desk. 'I want what you want. What every newspaper reader in this country not too hypocritical to admit it wants. I want the wet details on McGovern. Everyfreakingthing. Who is the stooper and who is the stabber. The name of everybody who has been up McGovern's arse. I want the guy sliced open like a mango. And I want it first. Forget anything you might have been planning to do in the next week. The dentist, the vasectomy, the new bed from Ikea, the bunk-up with that slapper you met round the wine-bar, the cosy anniversary dinner in your local tandoori. I want it now! Like . . . *yesterday*. We're going all-balls-out on this one.'

There was a stampede in the direction of the cashiers on the third floor with advance expenses chits – pink, carbontriplicated, clammy. The office-bound got busy with lists and photocopies of the relevant cuts (the McGovern file ran to four bumper packets then, probably twice that now) and maps and multicoloured charts.

Tame rent-boys, squat-heads, squealers and showbiz deep-throats were summoned by phone. Reporters were assigned to chase down McGovern's children, his children's friends, their friends' friends, their teachers, his heli-chauffeur, drivers, gardeners, pool-cleaners, housekeepers, roadsweepers, the waiters at the restaurants where he kept an account, make-up girls at the BBC, BBC commissionaires, bar staff, the disc-jockeys working on the radio station he'd put together the consortium to launch, the partners in his video business. Plough the fields and scatter. The hounds were unleashed. There were posses, ambushes, false trails, cut-offs; minor deception, fraud, cat-burglary in the public interest. It was zoo-time.

I spent the first five days in a leafy suburb of Stoke-on-Trent where the streets were named for Robin Hood and His Merrie Men – Nottingham Drive, Robin Circle, Maid Marian Lane – part of the pack doorstepping Peggy Askam, the mother-in-law. She lived in Alan-A-Dale Crescent, in a neat and trim house set back a good distance from the road, with plenty of trees.

Half a street away there was a neighbourhood park with a brook flowing through it, flowers and benches, swings and other jungle gym equipment, and tennis courts for the older children and grown-ups. You have no idea how long the long suburban day can be until you have spent one in a place like this. The only break in the monotony was a neighbour arriving at the side-door of Peggy Askam's house with food covered over by a tea-towel in case we might want to snatch a picture of that as well. Our own on-the-job food needs were taken care of by Genaro from the Appenines who sold hot-dogs and breaded drum-sticks at five pounds a pop from a trailer with tudor-timbered sides.

A few years earlier, while her husband was fighting the illness which finally killed him, Peggy Askam had been done for shoplifting – walking out of her village shop with a carton of Fairy Liquid and a jar of Nescafé that she hadn't paid for – and of course we gave all that another go around. She had a choice: talk to us about her daughter and her daughter's life with Scott McGovern, or have her own criminal past resurrected, only used big across the front page this time. The curtains remained drawn. A melanin-mapped hand reached round the door to fumble the milk in. She kept her counsel. So we treated the shoplifting story to a retread (further investigation revealed there had been a third item, a half-pound pack of Kerry Gold) and put it back on the road again.

After five days, and not much to show for it, I was reeled in and put onto a tale being peddled by the mouthpiece of a security and surveillance firm in south London who claimed to be representing the owner of a set of incriminating – 'well detrimental' – letters written to him by McGovern. This contact wasn't entirely without form: prison paintings by famous murderers, Bobby Moore post-mortem pictures, tapes that proved that Elvis really was working as a super-market bagger in Biloxi or Trenton, New Jersey – 'You're gonna hear Elvis Himselvis' . . . He had made efforts to off-load all of these in the past.

We met for lunch at the White Tower (his choice – he is a glutton for the taramasalata and the duck stuffed with cracked wheat and nuts. 'Reckon you can spunk a ton on me for a lunch,' he'd said. 'Least you can do.'). We were into the second bottle of retsina, and he was beginning to give me his palaver when – it had only taken me seven days, and total, round-the-clock immersion in the McGovern story to come up with this – I remembered that once, many years ago, I had interviewed Scott McGovern at his house; that there was probably still a tape of the conversation mouldering away in a drawer among my souvenirs.

This had been in the days when I seemed to have both feet set firmly on the up escalator and was establishing a reputation for juicing slightly more out of hardened interviewees than they were planning to tell. Zaire actually hadn't done me any harm. It had got me noticed. By about 1977 my strike-rate was among the best on the paper. I was a young family man in my thirties with an occasional picture byline, hungry, crashing my gears, working round the clock.

Aphasia – sudden black-hole amnesia – along with dizziness, anxiousness, a tingling in the fingers of my right hand, is one of the symptoms of the *petit mal* that has brought me down. But my memory of the – until then – lost afternoon spent doing the business on Scott McGovern came to me in a flash of what still feels like God-given recall. The sunny drive west out of London, the village with the ancient petrol pumps standing at its centre, the wrong turnings, the newly painted finger-posts, the winding track up to the house, the house's yellow clay wattle-and-daub exterior walls, the hollowed herringbone-pattern brick floors, the kelims, the dried hydrangeas in the China-blue vases, the dogs, McGovern's young friend William (not a T-shirt adonis or muscled love-boy, but a wire-glasses-wearing, pudgy, film-buff, Proms-going type) snipping flowers in the garden with a secateur.

There was tea made by McGovern himself. Then wine. Then a bit of pot. Then some nose candy in a poppy field at the back of the house with Murray, a harlequin Great Dane, crashing carelessly around, raising butterflies like dead cells beaten out of a mattress, flattening paths through the heavy-headed flowers. It was at this point that McGovern, sitting samurai-fashion opposite me on his knees, started crying big, perfectly tear-shaped, viscid, slow-rolling tears. It was something I promised not to mention and, until a week ago, had remained something I'd kept the lid on for fourteen years. With dusk there was more wine, and a leaving kiss full on the mouth which seemed natural at the time and doesn't feel at all unnatural now.

After transcribing it, omitting the part he had asked – pleaded with me, really – to keep to myself, I put the Scott McGovern tape in a desk drawer along with all the others and, as with the others, forgot about it.

For many years I saved the tapes, thinking that one day I might offer them to an archive or centre of national resource or, depending on how I was fixed financially, use them to cushion me in my lonely, sclerotic old age. Just recently, though, I have started to systematically over-record; have started, that is, to lay one gloomy ghostly presence over another, wiping the past. I am aware that this also represents an act of self-erasure, and that that is preferable in almost all ways to the self-effacement that turns out now to have been my interviewing manner – the punctuating phoney laugh, the conscientiously faked-up attitude of care and concern. I have been actively engaged in the eradication of this younger self adrift in another life, entombed in the dull lubricated brown ribbons of tape.

Many voices on the tapes belong to people who have

passed on, passed over, have become dead parrots. Scott McGovern is dying of an acute haematoma and lacerations of the skull – an unstill package, ventilated, evacuated, fibrillated, palpated, catheterised in his polyurethane plastic tent. Lidded eyes scanning the ceiling in coma vigil; muttering delirium; hot, flaccid fingers picking incessantly at the topsheet; the degradation of tissue; the vital centres irretrievably shutting down. (Entering the darkness; seeing the light; entering the light.) A modern death in a tiled hospital room.

And yet I was in a position to rewind McGovern to a place in his life – a balmy evening of acapulco gold and sangria, the dogs curled up asleep half on top of one another, William making gaspacho, and then his earnest, comfortable presence in Scott's canopied Jacobean four-poster – when he seemed inured to unconsciousness and coma and death. Would there be anything in his voice to suggest he could have suspected that blunt-force trauma might be one of life's surprises waiting further down the road? Any intimation that, deep down, at some hidden level, he suspected that violent death – shards of skull penetrating the brain's blancmange-like mass, like party wafers; blood vessels contused beyond recognition – was the card he was going to draw?

Each interview encounter is prefaced by a few inches of test tape, an acknowledgement of the operator's – my – constant tape-recorder angst. Often the space is filled by the sound of my own voice counting one-two-three-four-blah-blah-blah. Or, if a little drunk (in recent years my usual interviewing condition, no matter how early the hour), a few bars of a bearded old singer-songwriter favourite – something by James Taylor possibly, or 'Blue'-period Joni Mitchell ('The Last Time I Saw Richard', 'This Flight Tonight', more often 'Blue', songs heavily featured on my marriage's melancholic soundtrack).

On many occasions I have made sure the thing is working by recording a snatch of something from a hotel-room television or radio, the juke box in a pub, the air gusting into a taxi, clotted conversational hubbub, the rumble of a train.

Why is it, I wonder, that these noises, and the accidental, everyday background noises intruding on it once the interview is underway – a door opening or closing, a child calling, a clock striking, an ice-cream van's chimes, footsteps on a loose floorboard, the clink of cups or glasses, a telephone starting to ring and then being picked up in another room, a window blind unexpectedly snapping up – seem to be a truer record, to hold more of the moment, seem mysterious and powerfully charged, while the words sliding by in the foreground are without exception now as interesting as a wall of wet paint?

I found the tape with Scott McGovern's name on it and slipped it into the machine. I heard country sounds – birds singing, the rustle of trees – followed by the pages of a road-map being turned. I fast-forwarded and let the tape run for a couple of minutes until, ignoring the conversation, I recognised the rattle of sangria being poured from the Scandinavian glass jug. I turned the tape over and from the weak halo of echo around the sound could tell the interview was still taking place indoors. I FF-ed again, and when I pressed 'Play' knew that by now we were out in the field: Murray, long ago boiled down into fish-glue, could be heard barking in the distance. 'There were times when I got frightened. Things weren't going right, so I just went out and got shit-faced. That's me,' Scott McGovern was saying. 'Something goes wrong, I find a bottle. I don't like it about myself but I've done it before and I'll do it again.' There was the sound of him drawing cocaine up into his nose through a strip of magazine page rolled into a narrow tube, and then a protracted silence. And then it started, low at first. The choking sounds. The dry heaves. The wracked sobbing.

I picked up the phone and, after some stonewalling at his end by Betty Cooper, doing her usual impeccable job of running interference for him, made an urgent appointment to come in and see Howie Dosson with my unburied treasure in the morning.

A year ago, the paper joined the exodus from Fleet Street and moved into a speculative office-retail development south of the river into which has been crammed all the apparatus of a post-Wapping world where everything runs faster, does more, has a longer battery life and costs less. Air that hums and 7-Eleven lighting; trees that arrived in vans, delivered horizontally; escalators that glide noiselessly towards sylvan snacking areas where cashless payment systems wait to disgorge chicken-tikka-mayo-mint, Twix, Bio yoghurt (contains Simplesse), Filtafresh coffee. Elevated pedways. Perspex modules rising like bubbles. Water pleating down treated walls. Laminate signs with sub-surface graphics. Pro-Tekt travertine floors.

And on the main editorial floor, only more of the same: whiteness and work-stations, complex information networks and database systems connected together by wires and modems; half-litre bottles of Evian thrumming cleanly in unison. And – eeriest of all – the stillness; the hospital hush, invaded only by the ambient tap and click, the sound of the new newspaper office working.

'Mornin', Dust,' Des on Zone Red F (for 'front') Security

said as the glass doors whispered closed behind me. 'Chalky' White, 'Nobby' Clark, 'Spokey' Wheeler, 'Happy' Day, 'Dusty' Miller. The names of yeoman England. Names that have gone the way of butts of sack and the closed-shop and the nine-hour lunch. Des is the only person left alive who calls me this.

'Know what they say, don'tcha?' he called after me, as I fed my computer card into the turnstile post, not releasing it until I experienced that second of sensuous electronic suck or tug. 'We're practically looking at the world being linked by a fibresphere of almost incalculable capacity and efficiency. These new erbium-doped amplifiers will flash information of any size between machines at lightning speed. An ultimate realisable capacity of 75,000 gigahertz apparently, with an exponential rise in mips and terraflops and available band-widths.'

As the escalator wafted me skywards through the atrium, I tried to decide whether this meant that even Des – good old nig-nog hating, leftie-baiting, council house-owning, queer-bashing Des – had gone native, and discovered irony. Then I stole a look back at him in his designer coop-cum-scullery – the electric kettle with its calcium scabbing, the packets of Hobnobs and coconut creams, the ballpoint secured to the visitors' book with string and a yellow goitre of sticky tape, the marble counter stained to the colour of the back of his underpants by roll-your-owns and puddled coffee, the industrially soiled serge of his brown-with-ochre-trim livery – and decided: probably not.

'Newsplex' a fluorescent plexiglass sign says over the office entrance. It is in the same cosmic blue and the same stylised letters as the signs that hang over the (mostly untenanted) retail units on the lower levels. (So far the only items you can buy there are Nepalese fire lions, 'Bo Bangles', scented candles and forty varieties of nut.)

I watched a light on the motion detector glow red and the video camera turn silently on its mount as Kathy on reception depressed the concealed button to admit me to work. (Like sikhs and their turbans and men wearing shorts at their desks in summer, Kathy, a rap artist with a building reputation in the clubs, has received special permission to use the reverse-K on her identity patch in this way. 'I like it,' she told me the one time I brought it up, 'because it's more like, Hey, get out of my face. You know?'). As usual, I braced myself for an electrostatic shock from the anodised aluminium doorhandle in the shape of a cornucopia, and as usual I failed to get one.

Howie Dosson was watching golf. The vertical blinds around his office were louvred open and a small figure was making the lonely walk along a rain-lashed fairway. But the hundred feet between where Tosser was sitting and I was standing was filled with something that was as much New Age encampment or squatter settlement, Peruvian *barriada* or Tunisian soukh, as the editorial floor of a national newspaper.

The brave vision of Boyd Allen and Partners, the archi-tects, had failed to take into account the fact that the light streaming in through the ziggurat curtain walls, at the same time as achieving their aim of rendering the building trans-parent from the street, would also wash out the screens of the visual display units and fry the operators alive where they were sitting.

As a result, sheets, blankets, tarpaulins, squares of news-paper and anything else that might deflect light and heat have been gaffer-taped to the windows, creating a constant feral dusk. People sit in isolated mandalas of light with pyramid ionisers and personal air-deodorisers and cheap Korean plastic fans, insulated from the unpredictable forces eddying around them in the darkness.

The conditions, and the increasingly wildfire rumour that the present clean-desk policy is soon to give way to a no-desk policy (the 'non-territorial office' and 'hot-desking' are the new words we are currently hearing) have brought out something unmistakably tribal and primitive. The blocky inertness of many people's computer terminals has been enlivened with post-it notes and picture postcards and bills and bumper stickers and every manner of printed ephemera, as well as Christmas cracker thingumajigs and furry little creatures wearing vests with slogans like 'You're no bunny til some bunny loves you' and 'Hug me, I'm dirty', and rock star pictures and football pennants and Garfields delivering cutesy messages of love and hope. The terminals have taken on the funk-spiritual look of Third World shrines or the worship sites of some plump, bug-eyed folk deity.

The screens of the terminals that were logged-on but unattended showed hypnotic, swirling, maze-like patterns traditionally associated with ritual, trance, meditation: meteors, spermatozoa, polygons, spirogyra, Escher birds, the patterns you see when you're punched or nutted into a lamp-post, tumbling vectors and arcs and sacristy-coloured twill weave, shoals of weird reflective neon-patterned fish swimming in the electromagnetic radiation.

And materialising out of the real world chiaroscuro – formidable uniformed women with cover-girl smiles and airy spraywork hair, remnants of the American trainer/hostess teams, the Shandies and Mindies and Candies, brought in to help us confront the 'informational isolation' and insecurity we are programmed to feel when confronted with the new technologies; plus, tufted, leather-armoured motor-bike messengers as scary as Bantu or Yoruba. If I hadn't been drinking I'd have thought I'd been drinking.

In the outer office, Betty Cooper was on the phone talking to Tosser Dosson's wife about the new holiday outfits they were planning for him and looking like a subsidiary character in the early, black-and-white days of *Coronation Street* whose name I never knew but who was eventually killed off, although the actress, I believe, is still living. (The resemblance resides mainly in the area of the hair and the lightly salted-and-peppered upper lip and the enormous come-rest-your-head grandmotherly bosoms.)

The effect aimed for (and achieved) in Howie Dosson's inner sanctum is briary Rotary Club suburban: deep-polished cherrywood desk and conference table; leather-framed family pictures and award certificates and citations; deep-pile blue rug with oriental motifing; miniature raked Zen pebble garden; low suspension ceiling; high-street stereo stacker system.

He always seems happier, less challenged away from all this, though, in the part of the office with the synthetic carpet tiles and unit seating and chipped and beaten smoked-glass table. Designated the 'meeting module', this area is mainly used for watching sport on television. Which is what he was doing when Betty Cooper, still mulling over the men's beachwear possibilities at Jaeger with Brittany Dosson (the second, trophy wife), nodded me through.

The television is mounted on a metal bracket high in a corner and, viewed from behind, which is how I was viewing them, Dosson and the two men with him looked like figures in a betting shop waiting for the off, or business passengers in the departure area of an airport on one of the remoter

Scottish islands, anxious to get home to pick up the strands of their unravelling lives. This thought was probably prompted by the fact that they were standing watching a golf tournament that was taking place in a setting of craggy rocks and crashing waves and vicious dive-bombing gulls. On the screen was a man wearing plastic over-trousers, like something the elderly might wear for incontinence, inflated by the wind. He kept addressing the ball, and then pulling back from what looked like an easy chip with the six-iron. 'For fuck sake,' Dosson said. 'Jeezus. Shit or get off the pot.' And then, noticing me: 'And here he is' (I had the feeling he had rehearsed this) ' – the Norman Mailer of The Dog and Trumpet.'

The level of light in Tosser's office, because it is properly ventilated and blinded, was normal. But coming into it from the tarpaulined shanty town twilight, it seemed forensically over-lit. The light picked up the comb-through colouring in his hair and the perspiration shining his scalp and the metal filaments in his tie and trousers. He was wearing the button-down shirt (white, in his case) which is virtually generic in our profession, and the Windsor knot which, while strictly speaking proportionately too big, helps convey a useful sense of on-kilterness and symmetry and balance even when three bottles of Pomeroy to the good. His tie was a patriotic Manchester Olympics freebie. His suit – grey with an almost imperceptible window-pane check – was from the Savoy Taylors Guild. His shoes were a pair of the tassled loafers that his wife and Betty Cooper between them have probably decided give him that casual, careless, club-class, country-club ambience.

With Dosson was his deputy, Ronnie Duncan, hair still damp from his morning run into the office with his driver following in case his cruciate ligament should go again or anything urgent should come over on the car phone. With the exception of the tie, he was dressed more or less identically to Dosson; they shared a version of the same shag-edged, high-backed fringe, from behind rising cliff-like above the same lake of freckle-flecked, rippled pink pate. They were a double-act, a familiar duo: two big men taking manly pisses shoulder to shoulder in the toilets of expensive restaurants at the conclusion of my-way-or-the-highway, stainless-steel-balled, conspiratorial lunches. (Yeah let's go the extra grappa.)

The other person present was younger, shorter, fidgetier, balder. One of a recent graduate intake, Sebastian or Dominic-something had turned up on his first day wearing a flamboyant coloured shirt and slicked-up hair. But, immediately feeling the lash of Tosser's aversion to – terror of – anything that might suggest 'turd burglars' or 'botty bandits' – 'Watch out, folks!' he had bellowed across the newsroom, sighting the FNG (Fucking New Guy), 'There's a botty bandit about!' – had rapidly changed his style.

Permanently traumatised, perhaps, Sebastian-Dominic now had a set of exaggeratedly 'masculine' mannerisms – hearty yankings at his signet ring, staccato shootings of his cuffs, jacket-hitching rollings of his shoulders, jerking the corners of his mouth around, tough-guy fashion, between sentences – that made him look like an American borscht-belt comedian or Eurovision-vintage Cliff Richard. He had on a lightweight seersucker jacket and undemonstrative shirt and tie, and was wearing his hair in a way that admitted allegiance to none of the pariah groups or youth cults that the paper earns its reader-loyalty by ritualistically kicking seven kinds of shit out of. He was fragranced, focused, neatokeeno, with a tiny, light-seducing pin-hole in the burning lobe of his left ear.

'Why are they all shirt-lifters or skirt-lifters?' Dosson said, more or less as a reflex, as soon as the reason for my appointment, and the subject of Scott McGovern, was broached. He lounged with his legs stretched out on the seats in front of him where he could go on watching the television; the three of us took our places on the other, shorter leg of the 'L'. 'We'd all smelled the elephant shit behind that big-top,' Tosser continued, which in his case certainly wasn't true.

Scott McGovern had never made any secret of his affairs with men. It was common knowledge in the circles in which he moved. Some of these circles also occasionally included Howie Dosson: the two of them had met periodically at the annual industry bun-fights and blow-outs, and at cocktail parties at Number 10; they had been David Frost's lunch guests in his box at Lord's and had both clocked up the requisite number of appearances at high-profile charity events. But it had never occurred to Dosson that Scott McGovern was a kidney wiper. How could he be? He had none of the limp-wristed, cartoon kidney-wiper characteristics. His handshake was dry and strong, his clothes unshowy, his back straight. He was married like himself, with two children. Apart from the obvious circulation-boosting reasons, this was partly why Tosser had got his teeth sunk so deep into the red meat of the McGovern story. He felt personally traduced; that he had been left looking like an idiot.

He got up and closed the door to shield Betty's ears from something she was going to be able to read in the paper twenty-four hours later. Revealed on the wall behind it was a punch-printed blue-metal sign: 'Due to the AIDS crisis you are no longer required to kiss the boss's arse.' 'Okay,' he said. 'I suppose you can't inspect a sewer without wading through shit. Give us a listen of this twisted bollocks.'

All three of them kept watching the television, whose sound was down, and on which a bearded man in a tam-o'-shanter was preparing to tee-off, while I walked to the other end of the room and loaded the tape. The computer screen on Dosson's desk contained a list of words that seemed to have their beginnings or ends missing.

THETA
DIV
DOWNTO
ELSE
EOLN
MAXINT
OOLE
ORD
PRED
SUCC
TRUNC
VAR

They reminded me of T-shirt slogans glimpsed in the spaces between open jackets and shirts. Kathy on reception had been wearing one. I could remember it. It went:

utif
ngst
BB9

The first sound that came out of the speakers was Scott McGovern snorting coke – high-pitched, more of a whistle, followed by a long, satisfied, bone-clean exhalation. Then the out-of-doors country sounds. Then the mounting choking and sobbing. Then the wild track again – a breeze sifting through the tall grass in the meadow, a can being crunched, the dog's barks echoing down the valley. This contradicted the fierceness of the weather on the television in a way that all of us I think found unsettling.

Scott McGovern's voice when it came seemed unconnected to the world of wind and weather. It was coming from the world of machine-assisted bodily function and progressive structural dissolution and the agonal event, telling us what the daily reported spectacles of death and destruction – the meat-and-potato cases of kidnap, torture, murder and mutilation – repeatedly told us: that only other people died.

'My father made me suck his cock almost every day. My mother knew about it and she did nothing.' McGovern had recovered himself by this point. He was quite matter-of-fact.

'Oh *nice*. Oh very nice,' Dosson said, double-checking with a glance at the door that this was something Betty wasn't going to be able to hear.

'I can't drink any white liquids now,' the voice on the tape continued. 'They make me throw up. What I remember more than the taste of my father's come, is the overwhelming feeling of helplessness, of . . . '

'Oh fuck me while I'm sleeping. Oh *dear* oh dear.' Dosson was dividing his attention between the tape and the television, listening, pacing.

'I remember how I would always close my eyes as the cock

was in my mouth and he would start hitting me in the back and yelling "Open your eyes, you cocksucker!" '

'Walk in, aim the blade, build the grip . . . The angle of the spine is of paramount importance,' Dosson said. He was in the centre of the room, bent at the knees, sitting well back in his stance as the manuals recommended, air golfing. 'He's going to miss it. Got to . . . WhadItellya.'

'I was being controlled and humiliated by this man who was supposed to love me as a father. He would make me say that I wanted to suck his cock before he put it in my mouth.'

'The rotter,' Dosson said, indicating with a jerk of his head to me that he had heard enough. 'What a fucking rotter . . . Yeah well. Well done, Norm. How long has it took you? Only a week.'

'A week of being ripped to the tits,' Ronnie Duncan said under his breath. Sebastian-Dominic smirked and went to town on the ring on his little finger.

'We'll make an inky-finger out of you yet,' Dosson continued to me. 'Keeps the pot on the boil at the *very* least. So? What's all the long faces for? Let's run with it. Tone it down a bit. The language. Big sidebar on child abuse. "The menace stalking our children. What you can do if you suspect da-dee-da." Plenty white space in the lay-out. Get some oxygen in. Cheery fucking tale.'

The list on Dosson's computer had flinched and scrolled up two new words.

UNGLE
VETCH

Sebastian-Dominic undid his top button and loosened the

35

knot of his tie with one hand in a single action. Ronnie Duncan said he needed to stay for a word about the complaints that somebody was cooking sausages on the coals in the staff sauna again. Betty Cooper appeared in the doorway making signs that indicated that calls were stacking up and lunch was looming. 'I think we could do with a couple of blasts of your air-freshener in here,' Dosson told her. 'Haven't got any mind-freshener, while you're at it?'

Easing past her, I felt like somebody coming out of a strip joint into the daylight on a street where he might easily meet somebody he knows. 'Don't worry about the fucking writing,' Tosser called after me when I'd emerged far enough for the senior cronies camped within his power orbit to hear. 'We've got subs to do that bit.'

Sebastian-Dominic, still convinced that it was amusing – camp or kitsch or postmodern – to be slumming for a while on one of the tabs, was the first to laugh. 'If you lie down with dogs, you get up with fleas.' There was a chance he knew the expression. But I could see he was sure that wasn't going to happen to him, much as I had been certain many years ago that it wasn't going to happen to me.

The **SICKENING DETAILS** of Scott McGovern's abuse at the hands of his father ran as a splash complete with front-page barkers and screamers, and continued inside on pages 2, 3, 10 and 11. That was last Thursday. In the five days since, there have been think pieces, leaders, a shrink writes, why-oh-whys, a steady stream of TV crews coming to the office to interview Tosser (who invariably gets Ronnie Duncan to do a stand-up for him), reader helplines, phone-in polls . . .

On Friday, I took receipt of a case of Teachers and a complimentary memo from the editor (my first) that I picked up and read at least a dozen times in the course of the day, and which, I am bound to admit, I have in one of my jacket pockets now.

It is the dogwatch of a Monday, and we are still dug in around St Saviour's, a raggle-taggle army, half-alerted for signs of unusual movement, big-name visitors who might provide a couple of inches, some scrap of tiding-over copy, waiting for Scott McGovern to die.

At noon on the first day, a spokesman for the hospital had emerged outside the main entrance with a bucking, resistant sheet of paper to inform the legions of the press who had assembled that they were in 'a totally persona non grata situation'. That earned him a big hand in the bar of the North Stafford Hotel in Stoke when the pack who were staking out Peggy Askam saw it later on television.

A number of us who were there that night are here now, coralled behind the police barriers on a busy street in Marylebone. The situation is undignified, but not what you would call soul-sapping. The mood in the press pen is good-natured, almost festive. Somebody has put up a hand-written sign: 'Warning: Do not rattle our cage. Do not feed the animals.'

Since the decimation of the Street, there aren't many opportunities to get together to exchange gossip, spread rumours, compute redundancy pay-offs, and job shop, unless you're a member of the Garrick, which none of us here are. Some people are playing rummy or backgammon, squatting on the ground on their primary-coloured, high-performance layers of Thinsulate and Polartec and Trail and Trek; a couple of bottles have been uncorked, a hip-flask or two is doing the rounds, an old smudger is brewing up chewy tea with a lethal-looking, battery-operated electric poker device. (He only has to produce it to prompt one of a series of running jokes about objects that Scott McGovern may or may not have taken up the shitter.)

At St Saviour's, the cleaners and porters arrive and depart; broad-beamed nurses and smock-wearing doctors, riding the high of sleep-deprivation, maintain their soap-operatic ebb and flow; the police mark the change of shift by shrugging into reflector vests; a blue emergency light strafes the dark rectangular valley; a siren wails; a portable beeps; a photographer exercises his power winders, speed finders, nicad chargers, angle finders, the Quantum Turbo powerpack on his belt, squeezes off some restless scatter shots. By now we are factored into the equation a cause for unease and disappointment when we fail to show up. We have moved in, found a rhythm, become part of the furniture of the area, all in the space of a little over two weeks.

But we are not the only spontaneous hutment of strangers to have claimed squatters' rights here. Sitting out this death or death situation under the maintenance-free, canopied frontage of the hospital opposite − a white, parabolic, membranous structure whose vast trusses resemble dinosaur skeletons − is a troupe, a tiller, a *greenham* of Scott McGovern fans.

Here are the women who have marked every birthday, every anniversary, every minor milestone in his long career with knitted sweaters, home-baked cakes, and Gucci wallets. Here too the women who have sent him half-pairs of split-crotch panties with their telephone numbers attached, lockets enclosing clumps of pubic hair and wadded cotton wool, video cassettes of themselves masturbating and gasping his name; here also the women with a frail, wintering, chemotherapy look who have left McGovern money in their wills and now know they must expect him to pre-decease them.

None of this is guesswork or conjecture. I know it because, in common with every other paper, we have let loose a girl reporter on them – a sympathetic sister who, without exception, has vavoomed in there and stitched them up like kippers.

Even from this distance I am able to recognise individual faces from their pictures – the ring-leaders, the hard-core, the women who have logged the most battlefield time, sitting under posters and sagging bed-sheet banners and giant multi-portraits of McGovern, each likeness flickeringly illuminated and garlanded like Shiva or Vishnu or some other great Sanskritic deity.

Since becoming mini-celebrities in their own right by appearing on television and in the magazines and papers, they have been awarded an increase in their caste privileges and are accorded the sort of veneration reserved for tribal elders. They take the places that are considered the most draught-free and least vulnerable to rain and fumes from the traffic; sandwiches and hot drinks are brought for them from the café; their pillows are plumped, their shoulders and chilblains massaged, their blankets straightened, their sleeping-bags unzipped and hung up to air. And they have responded royally by assuming some of the glamour conferred by the broadcast and printed image – their flesh seems tighter, their hair looks livelier, their make-up more vivid; they are looking as good as it is possible to look after two weeks of douching in a narrow toilet cubicle at the nearest greasy-spoon.

Throughout the day all the women take their turn waving signs at passing motorists that say 'Support the vigil – Hoot if you hate tabloid scum'. Every hoot is rewarded with cheers and lairy whistles from their side of the road, indifference or the finger from ours if we're awake and watching. At six, at the police's insistence, the signs are put away, and there then commences the communal humming of old Sunday School and 'Sing Something Simple'-style, middle-of-the-road Radio-2 fare. At about seven-thirty, which is about now, the murmer of praying begins, accompanied by the burning of incense and joss sticks, and then the waving of guttering candles and cigarette lighters above their heads while they sway together singing 'Sailing'. Sometimes a priest is present to lead them in prayer and console them in their darker moments. Always there are the cyclops lenses, the lights and strobes, an electronic news-gathering team with the member wearing the banks of beepers on his belt steering the camera-wielder by the waist towards images offering the highest valency of fatigue and fanaticism and ecstatic abandon.

Watching this vigil in the last few days has revived memories of old newsreels showing the pre-dawn vigils that traditionally took place outside prisons in the hours before a hanging. The civically monumental, weather-chewed, Victorian façade; the watchers at the prison gates, waiting for the striking of the clock; the abolitionists' singing of 'Abide with Me' in the face of the jeering of their opponents; the offering up of silent prayers, the fervently pawed crucifixes and rosaries, the clench-faced men of the cloth; the posting of the typed notice on the gate confirming that sammy has taken the drop; the sombre picture of the mother and wife/sister emerging from the last anguished farewell; the bible-black three-decker headlines in the lunchtime editions. (Dead Dead. Oooo-oo, oooo-oo . . .)

You couldn't fail. How were you going to fail? It was a circulation manager's wet-dream. It was a no-brainer. Callous, premeditated, icy-fingered death, with the cliff-hanger of a last-minute reprieve. Areyewshaw! It was counting down the days. With me: seven—six—five—four ... The last meal. The last wish. The condemned man's last on-the-lip-of-death letters, all malformed capitals and coloured inks, off-loaded in a Dutch auction at the pub around the corner as soon as the prison doctor had pronounced ...

Since the night McGovern was kyboshed with his Emmy or his Larry, his Tony or his Bafta, we have been adding up the days. (Piling on the readers.) Here we are at Day 19, and counting.

Day 19. More or less all the pops have settled on this as a simple graphic device, a way of signposting the **STRICKEN MCGOVERN** coverage. In our case, the count-up is twinned with a second element depicting two inch-high, blacked-in male figures joined at the elbow and the head and instantly recognisable as the logo-fied version of the moment Scott McGovern walked off the concourse at Victoria with the man thought to be his attacker.

The police released the single frame extracted from the surveillance footage three days after McGovern's body was found. It was reproduced and repeated and analysed so exhaustively in the first twenty-four hours – reoriented, cloned, sharpened, blurred – that it was stripped of its primal shock power almost immediately. Within a further twenty-four hours, it had evolved into an icon, a badge, an emblem for a story that hadn't sunk into the mulch with the other stories, but had already become established as a moment in the life of the culture/as a piece of folk memory.

The strange thing, as nobody has failed to point out, is that the picture of Scott McGovern arriving at his fate instantly seemed as familiar as the smell of their own farts to many of the millions who saw it. McGovern gripping another man's right hand and elbow with both his hands and leaning in close to the body as if to whisper something rib-tickling, scurrilous, confidential – this was something that could have been taken from any edition of Scott McGovern's popular Saturday-night talk show in the last three years. His signature way of welcoming his 'guests' was to get down from the carpeted platform where sofa and armchairs were arranged in the ritual chat-show formation and do this little bit of business with them as they walked out of the wings.

Exactly what got said in these few seconds of schmoozing was never the point: the point was that it symbolised the celebrity transaction, from which civilians were necessarily excluded. But, as you certainly don't need me to remind you, the subject of what transpired between McGovern and whoever he happened to be glad-handing on the edge of that circle of light has remained one of endless, and fruitless, speculation. It was his 'Rosebud'. 'It's my "Rosebud",' he would tell interviewers archly. Only the people who had been on his show could say for sure, and they weren't telling, because they knew that if they did tell the invitation to appear again would not be coming. The comparisons with the rules of etiquette observed in royal circles (to which he was no stranger) were ones that McGovern made no attempts to discourage. He was as big, if not more famous, than most of the people he was interviewing. It confirmed his standing as one of the three people in British television consistently able to deliver an across-the-board, demographically shred-ded, fifteen-million-plus, late-night audience.

The surveillance picture put out by the police is mono-chromatic and typically sooted, soft-edged, indistinct: small objects have disappeared or their shapes have become seriously distorted; the two men are as insubstantial as charred or whittled wood – shades, after-images, an aggregation of information fragments about to dematerialise completely. And yet Scott McGovern's every tic and blink and glance is so ingrained that he seems easily identifiable within the dark mosaic blur that we have to believe is him. It is as if he has been expelled from the world of high-resolution and clamant colour, from television's clean rooms, and cast back into pre-history, to the days of shadow-gazing, of ghosting and smudging and pictures that rolled and boiled and intermittently dissolved into crazy static. The world of drawn curtains and firelit rooms and glowing lines turning into moving pictures on moonmobile grey-green thick glass screens.

The other figure, the man whose hand McGovern is gripping (the hand that soon will hold the object that will kill him – there is no suspense: he will die, we hope before the story rots on the branch, before the inevitable public indifference, and then hostility, sets in); the man whose ear his head is inclining towards in his signature manner (to utter what inducement, what come-on, to which latitude of kinked, expensive sex? ... 'Rosebud! Rosebud!') – the second figure has been regenerated, retrieved and enhanced, pushed to the point of bitplane breakdown, pixel decay. But it remains a blot, a blank, a nebulous, nagging presence, a composite image of every man who walked onto the set of honey shag and oatmeal tweed to talk up his latest mini-series or true-life hostage drama, his just-out novel or album or turn-around single featuring some proud-nostrilled diva or half-forgotten French film actress of the fifties. It is a reminder that every day is filled with unsuspected and ingenious ways in which destruction and disaster can happen, and that these death stories become the only stories that we tell ourselves. Following the plot of other people's misfortunes gives us the only sense of community we know. Hey. Shit happens.

Wet or dry?

Ice and a slice?

A whisky and splash.

The Ding-dong's?

Bass in a thing with a handle – I need something to hang on to at my time of life.

The usual.

'Miss KP' emerging out of the slippery back-of-the-bar duvet of bagged peanuts.

Guest ploughman's. Guest sandwich. Guest sausage.

Okay. We have: Kung Po chive. Piccalilli enchilada. Deep-pan Bombay duck. Egg-fry guacamole. Fried-egg nan. Peshwari scruncheons with gerkin. Sweet-and-sour bap.

The sneaky guy at the bar keeping an eye on the bandit to see if it has dropped.

Pubworld. Publife. Lifeworld. The felt-fact of aliveness (with a chaser, a stiffener, a lager-top). I had been adrift from it for three, perhaps four hours. I was feeling the pangs when Myc Doohan piped up. 'There was a little chicken lived down on the farm. Do you think another drink would do us any harm?' Myc Doohan no longs drinks himself, as it happens. But since he has been on the wagon his best friend has been Mary Warner. It suffuses the fabric of his clothes, announces him, clings to him like a miasma. Sitting next to

Doohan you can get stoned on the smell of his jacket. I knew it was going to be him and I guessed what he was going to say. I inhaled him before he spoke.

Myc Doohan and I climbed the greasy pole together, working for rival papers – and came skidding down at about the same time, to bite the dust. But whereas my difficulties have been mainly in the head department, he has had to make himself available for major invasive procedures (liver, spleen, lung).

Two things I know about Myc Doohan: he wears a surgical corset, and cowboy boots with scuffed buckles on the side. The corset is because of the purple scar that starts at his sternum and does a sharp right at his navel; the boots are for the added inches. Myc isn't small – he's average height – but he believes he is, which is the same thing. The dope keeps his face an unhealthy underbelly green, so the broken veins and busted capillaries swirl in it like the red ripples in ice cream. There is a glowing nimbus of pale hairs fringing his slightly out-turned ears. Most nights will find him dry crawling the pubs along the river (his system speeding from the caffeine and artificial sweeteners in the chain-drunk Cokes, sugar-shocked), skimming stones across the dim water at Chiswick Mall.

When we detached ourselves from the pack some of the McGovern faithful called us by name, and whistled and jeered. I felt cocooned from them in Doohan's musty, barny, wolf-like scent, and as we walked I listed for him some of the odorous qualities associated with various well-known diseases: diphtheria emanates a sweetish smell; yellow fever's scent is reminiscent of a butcher shop; scrofula (which I have a touch of behind the ears and knees, most painfully between the fingers) has – appropriately – the aroma of stale beer;

typhoid fever smells like fresh-baked brown bread; diabetic coma is acid-fruity.

The walking teased out another few threads in the frayed bottoms of Doohan's trousers. It is a fine June night, sappy and benign, and we kept on walking past The Run Rabbit and The Captain Murderer, and came in here, to The Cherry and Fair Star, where we knew we wouldn't be left finger-painting patterns in the glass rings on the Formica and glumly staring at one another during the gaps in our flabby, fitful conversational work-out. We parked ourselves gratefully at the table where young Ashley Cann and old Walter Brand (once 'The man with a passport to the world' in the *News Chronicle*, former deputy editor of the *Reveille*) were chewing over new type fonts and the dear old, dead old days.

'Degenerate, Manson, Exocet, Dead History Bold, Skelter, Arbitrary,' Walter was saying. 'The Wellington, the Wig and Pen, Poppins, The Stab in the Back, The Top of the Tip, the back bar of the Harrow, Rhona's killer fry-ups at the Albion, the long bar at The Feathers, Auntie's where Rene the sexy landlady made sure the barmaids always had bosoms of great splendour, Little Alfie distributing the enemies after ten o'clock,' Ashley said, as usual off on his own trip.

It was like a harbourside tableau from the hand of some journeyman Victorian dauber: Walter in his cavalry twills, suede chukkas and lumpy Arran sweater, whiskery, grand-fatherly wise; Ashley in his Converse All-Stars and baseball cap with the 'I ♡ Cops' slogan, gangling, prone to facial skin eruption. 'The London Apprentice' or 'The Search For Knowledge'.

Ashley is twenty-two and in the grip of something he calls topophilia – the capacity for devotion to a place. He is an habitué of the rat-runs, warrens, courts, snack bars, public houses, drinking clubs and trysting places of what used to be Fleet Street. Like an elephant that knows where to go to die, led there by the memory of something that hasn't happened yet, Ashley is drawn compulsively to the building that Sir Edwin Lutyens designed for the Press Association and Reuters, to the black vitrolite and glass façade of the old *Express* headquarters, to Whitefriars Street and Bouverie Street and Wine Office Court, to the blackened shell of Northcliffe's Carmelite House.

Nobody knows where this fixation comes from. His father is a professor of music at Aberystwyth, and from an early age tried to steer Ashley towards playing drums in an experimental noise rock band. All the time he was filling the house with the sounds of Varese and Ives, John Cage, John Adams, and Terry Riley, though, Ashley was carrying out comparative analysis of type-faces and headline densities on the *Mirror* and the *Sun*, assessing the influence of graphic scanners and laser letterpress platemaking, and what their failure to penetrate the page signified vis à vis the emotional payload of a story and reader reification; inhaling the inks from enhanced and traditional rag newsprints and logging the results; annotating and cross-referencing the most common sites of victimage (the shabby alley thick with nettles and tall weeds for public assault; the neat front room in the quiet street for domestics).

He ran away from home for the first time at the age of twelve. He was found tucking into a steak and stout pie at the Cheshire Cheese, with a biography of 'the muckraker for God', W. T. Stead, open on the scub-top table in front of him. They brought him home and bombarded him with Webern, Sun Ra, MC5, but Ashley's destiny was set.

'Lee Howard,' Ashley will suddenly announce. 'Editor of the *Mirror* under Cudlipp, had a bottle of whisky on his desk from the moment he arrived, called everybody darling, grew alarmingly larger and larger until he could no longer get into a suit and wore a kaftan instead.' Or, 'Duncan "Tommy" Webb, the great investigator, somewhat dramatically protected at his desk by bullet-proof glass.' Or, in connection with some casual remark, 'A good page one, right-hand second lead, 24-point Century Bold across single column.'

'Tell me again,' Ashley said to Walter across the table in The Cherry and Fair Star, 'about the time you were interviewing the King of Greece.' It is a story that has attained folkloric status. Walter was interviewing the King; the King, alerted by something in his manner, asked to see his notes; Walter handed over a single page containing the drawing of a big black cat.

'Not that old chestnut,' Walter said. 'It's got whiskers on it by now.'

'But I'm trying to keep alive an oral tradition,' Ashley protested. 'I feel like Alan Lomax with his old Uer immortalising country blues and field hollers, the plangent picking of turbaned mammies and blind old black men in Mississippi and the Carolinas, Fletcher Henderson's seasick piano.'

We were joined just then by Annie (real name Honoraria) Jeffers, who had been changing in the lavatory. She was wearing ribbed black tights and heavy workboots with a denim jacket tied by the sleeves around her middle. Her hair was cropped and the stubble dyed white-blonde, with just the roots left dark. Her on-the-job-hackette's clothes were stuffed in a Schipol Duty Free bag, one of a collection she keeps in a clapped-out Nissan filled to the sun-roof with rubbish for recycling that she has been carrying round for months, the dark glass and the white glass, the newspapers and cans, sorted into bin-liner bags.

'The sex-pest boyfriend's still pursuing her,' Walter said.

'Yeah, filthy bastard,' Annie said. 'Let himself in yesterday and went off with some of my knickers.' She resat the small metal bolt that she wears in her right nostril during the off-duty hours. 'Binoculars trained on the front door, weeps and pleads with me in the street, trails round after me like a ragged medieval whatsit mendicant, bells me a hundred times a day. He's developed an ideational disturbance. I'm an object of unwanted attention. Features think it'll make eight hundred words.'

'He sees you when you're sleeping, he knows when you're awake, he knows if you've been bad or good dot, dot, dot,' Myc Doohan said. 'You can have that as an opening sentence. Take it. It's yours. Mine's another Coke.'

'Teale-green, citron, avocado, pumpkin. Approximately in that spectrum? Muted brights. Or were they black?' Ashley said. 'Lace with a gossamer undercolour? The incorporation of a pattern language capable of renewing the communicative power of the surface. Contour-cut to minimise VPL. What colour were they?'

'One plain white, one pair oysterbeige.' Accepting the offer of a light from Doohan, the flame flared briefly in the silver bearing of Annie's nose-bolt. 'Donna Karan, New York, bought as a present. "Dry-clean only" label in the back. Come *on*. I mean. Can you imagine?'

'My darling brown-arsed fuckbird.' This was me. I was three big vod-ton's in, expecting to fly. 'James Joyce to Nora. According to the recent cache of coprophilia turned up at the University of Tulsa in Oklahoma, or one of those places.'

'I am on the fringes of erotomania in a way,' Walter

volunteered. He was lifting his sweater and fumbling with the waistband of his trousers. He pouched out a couple of inches of peach silk between the buttons of his braces. 'It seemed natural to me that when my wife died last year I should wear her lovely silk knickers under my Y-fronts, summer and winter. I suppose it was intended as a tribute to her. I don't know anyone else who would do this! I remember her every day because of it.'

I waited for Ashley to chip in with something about private memory becoming largely subsumed in public spectacle, one of his specialised subjects, but he was busy keying data into a palmtop PC. 'Flong pages. Pie-ups. Moodies. Low-mist inks,' it said on the liquid crystal display. A member of the bar staff brought Walter his dinner – a white plate brimming with off-white foodstuffs: boiled potatoes, white loose-skinned chicken, pale beans sitting in a pale cornflour gravy, which the barman looped a trail of as he put the plate down.

Walter unfurled the utensils and tucked the red brewery napkin into the neck of his shirt, and we all involuntarily stopped to watch him eating, all projecting him into the same unhappy future of rubber undersheets, plastic bibs, maggot-infested leg wounds caused by the long-term neglect of the profit-creamers in charge of the private death-with-dignity institution where he will linger until the day comes for them to pat him on the face with a shovel. (Walter is well over retirement age but, on a paper where the average age on the editorial side has dipped to thirty-four, having somebody with Walter's road-miles around, as they expressed it to him, provides a bit of much-needed bottom. A few years earlier, they had worked out that it would cost them more to sack him and make a redundancy payment than to go on forking out for his salary.)

Guessing the tack our thoughts were taking (it couldn't have been difficult), Walter said: 'Being old doesn't necessarily mean a life that is sick, senile, sexless, spent or sessile. Spare me the caregivers and the nurturers ... Don't mind me.' Walter lifted the gravied chicken leg off the plate with the fingers of both hands. As he opened his mouth to receive it his face became simultaneously death-like and gruesomely vivid, aureoled in the white light of a motor-driven Nikon.

It was like time-to-go-time, when the house lights show up all the cigarette burns and smashed glasses, and the tide-lines of furtively discarded crap. There were islands of tough marsh grass on Walter's cheekbones that hadn't been discernible before; tundra in his nose; gristly knobs and plaques and bosses of flesh; deltic tangles of veins; white matter creaming in the corners of his curdled eyes. For a strobic second, he looked like a carbuncular, Arcimboldo portrait of himself, composed entirely of artichokes and radishes, celeriac and beets, plantains and ugly tubers. Chicken grease coursed through the clumps of whiskers he had missed while shaving, came together with saliva and tertiary rivulets of grease and drooled off the end of his chin.

Walter had become an exhibit in Heath Hawkins's on-going project which concentrates on media reptiles drinking and eating – 'on the gargle and in the trough' – and in general succeeds, as he had just succeeded with Walter, in making us look authentically reptilian: thickened skins; orbital protuberant eyes; flicking fly-catcher tongues. He believes the pictures symbolise the human appetite for the morbid, the salacious and the horrific which we are here to stoke up and feed.

'The continually stuffed body cannot see secret things,' Hawkins said. 'Isn't that what they say, Walter?'

'Heath Hawkins.' Ashley was excited. He had what appeared to be a rose-pink aura round his lanky frame. 'Specialities: bird decapitators, puppy stranglers, woman beaters, wife poisoners, child molesters . . . '

'Mr Click-clack-Kodak,' Heath Hawkins confirmed. 'Mutilations, torture, necrophilia, autopsies, bestiality, road accidents, work-site carnage, a good blaze . . . '

'The naked shaking animal,' Ashley said. 'Killings, atrocities, butchery, gore. The shameful and menacing experiences that show humanity at its worst. You believed in the beginning that there was a psychic shield. But as more people died, and more friends, you learned there was not. Best-known quote, after your car was hit by a hand-detonated mine set off at a distance by guerrillas: "It was as if I had been to my own funeral. I knew everything – who wrote, who called, who came, who didn't." Second most-famous: "I want to turmoil people. Take them out of that comfort zone," a clear echo of McCullin's, "I wanted to break the hearts and spirits of secure people." A child of privilege, your fascination with extreme violence is your attempt to know the world by knowing the worst it has to offer. Please state your current worldview in a way that would be suitable for a white-on-black, centre-leg pull-quote of fifty words or less.'

'My grandmother used to have a saying that when hell was full up, the dead will walk the earth,' Heath Hawkins said. 'We're seeing it now. They are the dead. Out there. In here. Look at them.'

Heath Hawkins looks like one of the ruined beauties of the West Coast white jazz scene of the forties and fifties: Art

Pepper, Stan Getz, Chet Baker after their best blowing days, even their junky jailbird days, were long behind them, and death was clearly on the horizon. He has greased-up, greying copper-bronze hair that falls forward in a scimitar shape when he is helling round getting images of suffering and ruination to stick to the film, and stone-washed vacant blue eyes. Tonight he's wearing a tonic suit with narrow trousers and a single-breasted jacket, and a T-shirt that says 'Fuct' across the front in the lettering of the 'Ford' logo. He has a knotted saffron-coloured cord around his neck, and a small, pendant black velvet draw-string bag. As usual, his hands are taped with the same plastic tape he uses to protect the body parts of his camera. Visible on his fingers, and on his face and neck, are the open skin lesions that cover the rest of his body; they are caused by a parasitic protozoa picked up a decade or more ago, transmitted by a genus of blow-fly in Salvador or Nicaragua or the Congo or the Lebanon or Guatemala or Biafra.

'So,' Hawkins says. 'How we all enjoying this latest gruesical? A gas, or what? All it's missing is a body. Still no smudges of the battered and broken, is there? I tell you, Norman, we got to get the fuck in there. Go team-handed. Smush up right in the guy's face. Bang off some snaps. It *behoves* me. I mean, a couple of hours after she'd croaked it, Monet was in there painting his old lady, getting down the blue and the yellow and the grey tonalities of death. And for sure he's feeling no pain, old McGovern. Not no way is he feeling any pain, right. He's pure, insensate vegetable matter. I enjoyed your piece by the way. Good going. But, listen. We've got to crash it, man. Do it. Go in with me. Run a raid on the factory of bad karma.'

Hawkins has become as habituated to hospitals as he once

was to famines and foreign wars. His first portfolio after he had hung up his flak jacket, his shrapnel-holed olive drabs, came together over the months he spent lurking in the Casualty Department of a busy inner-city hospital, homing in on torn flesh, screaming faces, meaty wounds, following his subjects into emergency surgery, prowling the morgue. The hospital management had to ask him to leave in the end.

He kept taking pictures of his first wife through her slow death from cancer; the ravages of chemotherapy, the bifurcated scar of the mastectomy blown up into images of high-contrast, extreme graininess.

He met Murrayl, his second wife, at a police scene-of-crime murder reconstruction in a town in the West Midlands. Bearing a strong resemblance to the murdered woman, Murrayl had volunteered to put on clothes similar to the ones the woman was wearing on the night she died, and follow the route from the commuter station to her home ten minutes' walk away that she was taking when she disappeared. Hawkins had approached Murrayl at the end of the photo call and a few days later persuaded her to lie down in the weed-choked alley adjacent to a Salvation Army Citadel where the body had been found. He photographed her with a supermarket carrier bag taped over her head and her clothing disturbed, resting against a bunch of flowers with a card that said, 'From regulars and staff at the Railway Inn. A tragic loss.' Murrayl went on to do some glamour modelling and, now separated from Heath, currently works as a nineteen-forties-costumed cinema usherette at the Museum of the Moving Image on the South Bank.

This time when Annie needs a light, Hawkins provides it with one of his best-known props: the veteran Zippo lighter with the inscription that reads, 'Though I walk through the Valley of the shadow of death I shall fear no evil, for I am the biggest bastard in the Valley.' I notice that Annie cups his gaffer-taped hand in a way she failed to do with Myc Doohan, a charged but tentative contact, like Billie or Ella putting the lock on an old RKO steam-radio mike. 'The left hand, which signifies unjustly the evil side of life,' Hawkins says, 'the sinister portion of space, the side from which we're told we mustn't come upon a corpse or an enemy, or a bird.' Annie briefly touches her cigarette to the tip of the wayward, sheeting flame, and excuses herself.

Hawkins takes a lens out of his camera satchel and removes it from its chamois-leather wrapping. It locks into the body of the Nikon with an important, finely engineered snap. He brings the camera to his eye and demonstrates the soundless, smooth, oil-on-oil movement of the lens as it is focused. Then he sets the camera down and proceeds to something that I have started to suspect is coming. He takes the black draw-string bag from around his neck, and sits back to wait for Annie's return.

The hands are the hands of a child, conceivably a baby: shrunken, dark-skinned, leathery-looking, the skin brought together where the wrists would be and secured with a metal band, like a blood sausage or a continental salami. Hawkins places the hands either side of the base of the glass from which Annie has been drinking, so that it looks like some shocked-to-your-socks appeal on behalf of the latest Third World drought and famine, or a sentimental Victorian funerary arrangement.

He has been here before. He waits for the tears to come, tracking down her freshened matte cheeks, over the no-make-up make-up of her spasming mouth, before snapping off the shot that casts her in the role of tragic wife, grieving mother; as participant now, rather than professional witness, dealing hands-off with the world, separate from what she sees.

'Let smiles cease. Let laughter flee,' Hawkins says. 'This is the place where everybody finds out who they are.'

The tiny hands, loosely fisted around the stem of the glass, are patinated with a close, mottled pattern of amber and black-brown translucent tones; they look almost like an out-growth of the laminate plastic surface of the table. I can see now that the glass-rings, far from being irregular or random, would form a pattern if reproduced over a larger area, and are an in-built part of the design.

Scott McGovern has attracted the inevitable cargo of loonies, the usual fruitcake fringe of clairvoyants, UFO spotters, astral seers, poison-pen letter writers, faith healers and intergallac-tic travellers. And, outside the hospital, some kind of demon-stration is going on. But it is impossible to tell from the silent, circling, grave-faced placard-carriers who or what they are demonstrating for or against. There is no 'Oggi-Oggi-Oggi'. No 'What do we want! – Peace! When do we want it! – Now!' No clown-painted children in pushchairs, no electric hailers. Just the dogged shuffle-tramp, and the slogans and daubings that I dutifully write down in the hope that they might arrange themselves into some narrative shape later.

'Health, beauty, morality'
'Stain, defilement, disorder'
'We live in the ecstasy of communication, and this ecstasy is obscene'

'I want to care but it's so hard'
'Upland fields, hilly roads, noble horses'
'Fame, packaging, standardisation, vacuity, death'
'The mouth kisses, the mouth spits — nobody mistakes the saliva of the first for the second'
'More imprisoned, lost and alienated than ever before'
'Unnerving in their absoluteness, their remoteness'
'These creatures of the electric limbo'
'BB9'

Heath Hawkins has his flashgun hooked up to the power-pack on his belt; he's ready to rumble. 'Okay. Let's blind the fuckers. Shish their fuckin' eyeballs, man,' he says.

Leaving by way of a side-street adjacent to the west wing of St Saviour's, I see the camera emplacements at an upper window, the fisheye and periscope and telephoto lenses trained on the magenta reflecting window of McGovern's room. The family of four who usually live there have been moved into the Regent Palace Hotel until the doctors pull the plugs.

'TV star Scott McGovern, who suffered massive brain damage after an attack at his home, died in hospital last night. Doctors switched off the 54-year-old stricken celebrity's life-support machine after his family said a poignant farewell.' The story is stroked into the system, slugged **strickceleb** for easy retrieval, ready to go.

T : W : O

There was once a velveteen rabbit, and in the beginning
he was really splendid. He was fat and bunchy, as a
rabbit should be; his coat was spotted brown and white,
he had real thread whiskers, and his ears were lined with
pink sateen. On Christmas morning, when he sat wedged
in the top of the Boy's stocking, with a sprig of holly
between his paws, the effect was charming.

My bed looks as though it has been pissed in, and the piss
has soaked up the sheets into the pillow, turning it a dirty
urine yellow. It hasn't (at least not lately). The yellowing
comes from the liquid inhalant I dose the pillow with at
night and whose piney menthol vapours do what little they
can to stop my furred tubes and pumps and passages packing
up on me completely while I'm sleeping.

'Karvol' to see me off; Meryl Streep to bring me round
again. I jam Streep's Talkingbook version of *The Velveteen
Rabbit* over my ears as soon as I am half-awake, to lull me
into consciousness.

If I associate this reading of the old nursery story with
happy landings, it is because the first time I heard it was
30,000 feet over the Atlantic, in the middle of one of those
electric storms that has the cabin staff shooting pop-eyed,
fixed-grin glances at one another for reassurance and pas-

sengers gasping audibly every time the plane pitches or plummets three hundred feet through a hole in the turbulence, up-ending sneaky movie-time Scotches and Virgin Marys. I was sitting next to a grey-haired granny, travelling alone, up in a plane for the first time, and being barmily unafraid about the fact that the sardine can in which we were strapped, helpless, was being jiggled about the sky like a coin in God's dark pocket.

I clamped on the headset and started whipping through the channels in search of comfort, help, distraction. I passed on the Chopin preludes, Horovitz in Moscow, Carl Sagan revealing the secrets of the cosmos, Dwight Yoakum, David Hamilton's *Chataround* and P.M. Dawn, stopping when I heard Streep's cod English-governess accent telling the tale of the velveteen rabbit against a light string-quartet and flute backing. The archaisms of the language of course were instantly lulling, and the Ice Maiden American voice doing battle with the intricacies of English pronunciation – 'reeelly splendid', 'a look of wisdom and bewt-ee', 'that was a waaanderful summer!' – provided a secondary diversion. I came in after the beginning of the story but, by the point where the Boy and the rabbit are tearfully separated after a bout of scarlet fever (I cried), I was engaged enough to feel as if a cooling hand had been laid across my fevered brow (the baby-pink manicured nails; the modest diamond solitaire). In my memory the hand has come to belong to Isabel, the hostess who earlier in the flight had assured me that the chest-pains I was experiencing were not signs of cardiac arrest but most likely the consequence of putting away too many sherbets the night before, and to keep on steadily sipping glasses of water.

I listened to *The Velveteen Rabbit* two or three more times all the way through before we landed. That was six years ago, and I have hardly stopped listening to it since – on the tube and in mean-curtained hotel rooms in early-to-bed towns; in pubs and during the purgatorial, drawn-out days of waiting at flower-heaped atrocity sites.

An Olympic sprinter once told me about the strange sweet feeling that ran through him at the moment he decided to accept God into his heart: 'Like cool air,' he said, 'being blown into my chest through a straw.' I suppose it could be something like this I am trying to capture with my twin pathologies or rituals: the astringent menthol vapours on my pillow at night; the crisp insinuating kindergartenisms of Meryl in the mornings. (The latter are experienced largely as sounds and abstract associations by now – compulsive, reveried, divorced from any story.)

I am living in what I suppose, looked at objectively, you would have to call reduced circumstances. But reduced from what? Reduced from how I used to live with my wife, Even, and our children, Tristan and Jennifer, certainly. For instance, the 'bed' is not a bed but a grubby tangle of bedding on a sofa: sometimes I clear it away when I leave; just as often I'm relieved to find it lying where I left it when I come home. Ditto the milk cartons and cups and kitchen things that officially live behind a counter in the same room, with the two-ring hotplate and the 'junior' fridge that over the years has taken several coats of paint.

This is a studio flat – i.e., one bedroom, one living room, one alcove kitchen, one lavatory with oppressive, entombing stall-shower. Two of the main items of furniture are light-weight and collapsible, and were probably meant to be tem-porary when they were first rescued from the pavement by my landlady, Mrs Norstrom: a garden recliner with a rusting frame and wipeable upholstery, covered in a pattern of big, blown red and orange flowers on a foxed-blue ground; an aluminium table with hinges down the middle where grease and crumbs and fugitive food scraps accumulate. There is one picture – a poster-photograph of the Brooklyn Bridge. Plus a copy of the Desiderata on a monkish parchment scroll that my daughter gave me as a present when I moved out of the house and in here about fifteen years ago, when she was seven. It used to remind me too much of recovery programmes and the 12-Stepper's 'Serenity prayer' ('It's embarrassing but it's beautiful') that somebody at the office once slipped anonymously onto my desk with a note saying it was time to forgive myself and get some self-esteem. For a long time I kept it turned face to the wall, with the words – 'Go placidly amidst the noise' et cetera – glooming out only when Jennifer visited me with her mother. The carpet is the kind of straw stuff placemats are made of in healthfood restaurants, the walls unobjectionable, indeterminate.

Very occasionally it can look as though Annie Jeffers has come with her recycling bags and dumped the contents in here. It's very far from 'Orderliness. Harmony/Piles of sheets in the wardrobe/Lavender in the linen'. Whoever it was said men know nothing or little of the 'wax' civilisation had a point. A man needs a maid.

I'll admit it (already have admitted it): I've lived better. But I've also lived worse. The back-to-back where I was born will do for openers, with the slop-bucket in the corner of the kitchen, no electricity, no hot water, lush fungal damp, the ceilings cracking and eventually caving in. This appeared to be nobody's fault, and certainly not ours. I was a war baby. We were living in a port town that had been a regular target for the Germans. Accommodation of any description was in short supply. We were no worse off, and probably considerably better off, than thousands of others.

My father had gone back to doing what he had been doing before the war. He was a cutter for a Jewish tailor, and every suit he ever wore was a three-piece, and every coat had real buttonholes on the sleeves. He was a big man with a slight stoop and honest brown curly hair who put his wage packet on the sideboard every Friday unopened. I used to go to the barber with him every other Saturday just for the times when 'Dickie' Ames cleaned the hair out of his clippers with a lighted wax taper: the sizzle of the hair igniting, the acrid burning smell among all the sweet smells of haircream and shampoo and dense glop. In his spare time my father made wallets and purses, and engraved cowboy scenes with lariats and prairie moons and cactuses onto wide leather belts, which were worn at weekends by a good number of his friends.

Later, when we'd been given a flat in one of the new blocks put up by the council, my mother went to work as a cleaner in some furniture shops and a pet shop in the town centre. I'd hear her going off in the mornings when it was still dark, the clattering of her high heels, and the heels of the two women who worked with her, echoing up to the fourteenth floor where I was still huddled in bed. Occasionally, I'd see the three women, usually with a couple of men in tow, going into one of the pubs on the edge of the fruit market just after opening time, although I don't think they ever saw me.

My father died suddenly of a brain haemorrhage when he was fifty-nine, only seven years older than I am now. I was in a hospital canteen interviewing a man whose wife had

62

just had both her legs blown off by a bomb planted in a litter-bin by the IRA when I was told, and the sudden reversal of roles was disorienting. The sympathy the man who I was interviewing showed me was different not just in degree, but in levels of spontaneity and compassion, to any I had shown him.

We buried my father in one of his own suits – a narrow chalk-stripe with double-breasted waistcoat with revers. The meat, his thumb and some of the fingers of his right hand were grooved almost to the bone from a lifetime of sewing and from the pressure of his leather-working tools. Almost the last thing I did before they put the lid on was explore with my own fingers the hatchings and depressions that were the most tangible evidence of who he had been. I remember, with the undertaker's men crowded respectfully behind me in the tiny bedroom, and a chink of very bright light blinking in through a gap in the curtains, trying to have a thought suitable to the moment. Instead, the words that teletyped through my brain were: Friends are still stunned . . . Parents are deeply shocked . . . Park officials are still visibly affected . . . The small town is mourning the deaths . . .

The years when I was married are the only time I have ever lived in a house – lived somewhere, that is, where the living rooms and the bedrooms are on different levels. Even had grown up in a house, the children were born into one, but in all the years I lived as part of a family with them, I never felt properly acclimated; never fully keyed in to rhythms of upstairs and down, to unexpected encounters on the landing, to the complex vertical traffic-flow. I never felt, in the fullest sense, intimately and absolutely *at home*, all guards down. Eventually this was to develop into feelings of anxiety and dread (and then resentment), so that home, far from giving me a protected corner in the world, a foothold in the universe, was in the end the last place I wanted to be.

For the first years, though, it was a normal young marrieds' nuclear existence. We were trailblazers in a part of Fulham that at that time (it was the early seventies) had yet to see its first Neighbourhood Watch window sticker or its first Montessori school. We lived in a three-bedroom house in a modest turn-of-the-century terrace that was soon fitted out with the stripped pine and the directors' chairs and the big ball Noguchi lanterns everybody (everybody like us, that is – the in-comers) had in those days. We had the William Morris curtains from Liberty, the knock-through lounge, the rectory table, the bookshelves-on-bricks.

The centre of operations, though, was the kitchen, where, in order for Even to go on earning her screw, we had installed a brick-base, butcher-top food preparation island and a restaurant-quality range. Even had been a food writer contributing mainly to part-works when we met. Our first conversation was about a piece on the best cuts of meat for a casserole that I was subbing. (She had written that Chicken Marengo was a dish created on the battlefield of Marengo. I wanted to know if there was any way of avoiding the repetition. She said there wasn't. The repetition stayed.) On the phone I had imagined somebody flaxen-haired, lantern-jawed, big-boned, an enthusiastic trencher-woman. But in the flesh, although tall, and attractively assertive, she turned out to be wiry, dark, with long straight hair and the witchy, peasant, close-set eyes of the Essex hinterlands, where she had grown up on the bait farm owned by her father.

Even was, as her name suggests, unruffleable. She had a sense of balance and equilibrium that was perfectly suited to working at home at the same time as bringing up two small children. She was employed as a tester for the food writers on a couple of weekly magazines (deracinated women with power shoulders and brutal breath who, so far as I could tell, didn't know a *bain-marie* from a bath bun), making sure before they were printed that the recipes for fish fritters or *pissaladière* didn't give the wrong amounts of this or that, or say 'braise for three hours' when what they meant was thirty minutes.

She was systematic, scientific, scrupulously weighing, measuring, sieving, skimming, boning. There was never the homely spot of flour on the nose, the frontierswoman dough up the arms to the elbows, the frivolous slogan or Bruges pissing boy made with the left-over pastry, egg-brushed on top of the pie-crust. She wore professional whites, surgical gloves, surrounded herself with things that glinted, pulverised and cut – meat basters, steak tenderisers, larding needles, jointing knives, shears – things that would have seemed as at home in an operating theatre as a kitchen.

In between times, she interviewed prospective au pairs responding to the ad we seemed to have more or less permanently placed in *The Lady* – the Finn, the Lapp, the stream of Filipinos, the endless Poles, the dumpling-faced girls from the north of England called Eileen who sat in their rooms at night crying, and then disappeared for mysterious operations, never to be seen again.

At least that is the way it all looked to me then, although I'm probably not the best witness. I was working on the subs' bench at the *Daily Express* and gradually acquiring what I have heard called that *interestingly used* Fleet Street look. The day theoretically started around lunchtime and ended at ten, but add on two or three hours either end for drinking and a little lifestyle feedback, and you'll see that I was missing in action for anything up to fourteen hours a day, on a daily basis.

In 1973, the year Jennifer was born (Tristan is two years older), I joined the 'quality' paper that was going to allow me to branch out and develop on the writing side. (I had moonlighted for them on a couple of stories while I was still subbing at the *Express*, and an editor there had liked what he'd seen.) I was in Zaire covering the Ali–Foreman circus after only about a year, and, within another year, was being indulged by the space barons on the sixth floor who were the men (they were all men) with the real power on the paper. I was prepared to go anywhere to write about anything and to stay there for as long as it took (admittedly this usually wasn't very long). On the strength of these background pieces and extended news features, I started doing profiles and then an occasional column with my picture next to it in which I was allowed to use 'I' for the first time (I found this very difficult).

I was often cranking out pieces for the home editor, the features editor and the op-ed page editor at the same time. In addition I was saying 'yes' and when I should have been saying 'no' to freelance commissions from one of the colour supplements and a number of monthly magazines. Then, because independent commercial radio had just been launched, and the people who ran the stations were finding twenty-four hours a lot of dead air to fill, I started providing opinions-by-the-yard on two-o'clock-in-the-morning phone-ins and round-the-table blah-blah shows, all for the price of the bus-fare home.

I went on well tanked-up and mouthed off about . . . oh who knows. This was the seventies. The Tate 'bricks' controversy. The Cambridge Rapist. The white wine explosion. Glam Rock. Stagflation. Were they the seventies? And then in addition there were the latenight, phonefreak old reliables. When does a foetus have the right to life? When can the plug be pulled? When can life be taken? Where does life exist outside our galaxy? How close to creating life dare we come? The modern Fagins who prey on homeless youngsters. The dangers of 'kit car' assembly packs – stuff I'd get up from a table – even my own table, even if there *were* people round, and even if Even *had* spent all day preparing the layered vegetable terrine in aspic and the Crème Senegale Roast Ribs of Beef we were eating, in a road-test for *Woman's World* – and go round to the pub to get away from.

For thirty-five years I had never known what it was like to be depressed or anxious. I cottoned on at an early age that ordinary life in an ordinary place on an ordinary day in the modern world is dreary. I also knew that the place to be to combat that dreariness, to get the best view of the mess that happens when the orderly arrangements of everyday life collapse, was at a newspaper. I knew that on newspapers the universal motto, although nobody might ever admit it, was: The worse it gets, the better I like it.

And for years I did like it – was cheerfully addicted to the charge of adrenalin once every twenty-four hours, the rumble of the presses throbbing through the building, the ink still wet on my name above a story, the scamulator blazing with all its lights on. But I was running on the rims by about 1977. Sometimes it seemed as if my head would burst – literally blow open, spraying all the opinions and punditry and Jack Daniels wisdom and sliced and diced philosophy, all the facts and data and life histories and geographies I spent all my time going around hoovering up from other people – kersplat! – up and down the walls.

There were warning signs, small things at first, that I chose to ignore. I boarded wrong trains – trains going somewhere other than I was supposed to be travelling – twice in the same week. I found myself penniless in a strange town, standing in front of a cash dispenser transfixed by the four-letter acronym LISA, which stood for Locally Integrated Software Architecture, but unable to remember my Personal Identification Number – four digits I had tapped out perhaps a thousand times in a sequence that I had assumed my body would always remember even when my mind couldn't. It was like forgetting how to dance or swim, or how to beckon to somebody or wave goodbye. My fingers fumbled out the wrong code twice, and the card was gobbled into the machine – the white-light hologram of a swan-in-flight fluttering bleakly through a spectrum of kingfisher blue to orange cadmium as it disappeared.

Increasingly I found myself with a single finger dreamily stroking the granularity of the number '5' on a touch-dial phone, that hard-locating nipple, while my memory refused to come up with numbers I had been dialling half my life. Going to a typewriter had always been an ordeal, but now it became an ordeal of a different order. I had known where to find the letters on a typewriter the way I knew where to find my limbs. But I'd have these fleeting memory seizures and I'd be aphasic, dyslexic. I'd feel the climbing panic, and then it became difficult to breathe. I couldn't have pecked out 'John sees Janet. Janet sees John' in those circumstances if my life depended on it. It was as if something in my motor memory was slipping or being worn down, or shorting out at increasing intervals, with no advance warning given. For some time they were eventless emergencies I was able to contain; there was no visible slide into melancholy, no crescendo of excitability. I was fine − until I wasn't. When it was over, nothing had happened.

I had always been a notorious stonecutter and deadline surfer − getting things in only minutes before they were due to go to press − but now I started missing deadlines for the first time. The transcription service hadn't got through the interview tape when they were supposed to, or had lost or mislaid the tape. Or I had been hanging around for hours waiting for the motorbike messenger to collect the copy (these were the days of slow-motion, terrestrial communication), and he hadn't shown up. Or the interviewee had failed to turn up at the restaurant/bar/other as arranged (shome mishtake). Or Even had given me a deadline for the wrong day when she took the message. I remember even trying to convince somebody that I'd left an article he had been expecting on his desk while he was away at lunch, and a gust must have flushed it through a window. Other people, the elements, something was always to blame.

The flak at first was internal: rumblings were heard; back staircase confabulations took place: memos were circulated. But then one or two of the people I had gone to interview wrote or called to object to my conduct. There was the 'alternative' comedian whose bottle of Remy (a present from his agent − it still had the bow on) I made heavy in-roads into after his flat-mate made the mistake of asking me in to wait; and the senior politician who received a call from the novelist I'd got wrecked with one lunchtime, inviting him to join us in the bar at Langan's rather than me going to the Department of Trade and Industry to interview him as arranged. ('Oh anyway who gives a fuck. I wouldn't give you the sweat off my balls to press your pants with,' the novelist said, when the MP made it clear that an afternoon getting shitfaced in Mayfair couldn't be shoe-horned into his very pressing programme.) On two other occasions around this time I remember being on my knees bleerily wiping traces of vomit off a fancy Staffordshire china toilet bowl, and poking bits of vomit down the plug-hole of a bidet with my pen, although I believe the owner of the toilet bowl was the only one who complained.

Obviously it couldn't go on indefinitely. Some sort of crunch-point was coming. When it happened, it happened in the garden of an English film actor whose name you would probably know, and the way it happened was this. I had driven down to the Thames-side mansion at Maidenhead with a photographer, and the photographer and the actor had gone into the house to assemble alternative outfits for the pictures. It was a hazy, overcast day, and I stayed outside to steal some nips from the quarter-bottle in my research wallet, and watch the river. I was sitting at a white antebellum table on a terrace flagged in pink-and-white chequerboard squares. There was a brightly painted Romany caravan half-way down the long lawn, and a red phone box, with a working telephone inside it (it rang once while I was sitting there, then stopped abruptly), by the swimming pool. Beyond the pool was a paddock with two ponies in it belonging to the actor's daughters, and some rustic, pony-sized show-jumping fences painted with red and white stripes. A stand of weeping willows acted as a kind of screen between the house and the river, where the occasional glassy-hulled cruiser nosed by.

I don't know how long I had been waiting on the terrace. I had been watching rabbits high up in a field on the other side of the river, and had lost any sense of time. When I heard the voice, I knew who I was but I wasn't very sure of my whereabouts. My heart started racing and my mouth was very dry; only by opening my mouth and gasping did I seem able to take in any air. The voice was behind me, and I knew that what it was saying was directed at me, and required a response; but I couldn't remember in whose garden I was sitting, or how I came to be there or – although it was a distinctive, in many ways familiar voice – whose voice it was. It was as if my brain had missed a beat, and then jammed.

A few nights earlier I had had an eerie experience in an Indian restaurant. I was sitting alone, eating a chicken curry with chapatis and dhal, when I noticed a sliver of glass in the food I was just about to put in my mouth. At the exact second of the discovery of the glass, and before I could even think about calling the waiter over, a brick was hurled through the window where I was sitting and glass rained onto everybody's food. It was as if time had somehow been turned inside out, and a tangible fragment of experience had been allowed to come in advance of itself.

During the period of the seizure in the actor's garden, I was neither back in the Indian restaurant nor in the garden itself but somewhere perplexingly – unpleasantly – in between. My adrenal glands were overworking, pushing my blood pressure up, and I was experiencing palpitations and rotating areas of colour in my peripheral vision. But when I could focus properly, and the nausea had stopped rising in my throat, I found myself in the middle of a polite conversation with a man wearing a sweat-shirt with the picture of a skier on it and the slogan 'Chamonix – Powder and Glory – Make madness a way of life' and sharp-edged creases in his jeans who seemed to sense nothing amiss.

I sleep-walked the interview like a trouper, then went home and put myself to bed and stayed there, like a rat in its hole, a rabbit in its burrow. I huddled up to myself imagining I was living in a hut in a forest with wolves sharpening their claws on the heavy granite slab that formed the doorstep, for most of the next five months. When I re-emerged, rubbish was piled shoulder-high in the streets, looking lacustrine at night with sodium light reflecting on the knotted and twist-tied sacks, and it was winter.

I had moved out of the house by mutual agreement a few weeks earlier and into my own place, where I still am all these many years on. It was a lucky arrangement, as it turned out: the family was a few streets away and, although for a while the children were afraid to be in the company of their shaggy and dead-eyed daddy, Even had a key so that, in the darkest days of my sadness of the spirit, she could come round and minister. She arrived and departed silently, leaving bread, milk, butter, eggs; and occasionally I'd hear her lifting objects to dust them as I lay in the next room doped, diasopan-ed, chemically coshed out.

The company quack rated me as no more than a heavy social drinker and put my malaise down to 'overstimulation' and overwork. The paper kept me on half-pay. During the day I mooched about, masturbated – masturbated compulsively for a time: standing up, sitting down, on the toilet, in the shower, probably a classic symptom of self-estrangement and dread. Mostly though I lay on the sofa and watched the play of light from the television on the ceiling and walls – the flashing electric tints; the numinous sheen; the monochrome shadows like residues or traces, like racing clouds.

I came to look forward to a programme which repackaged old Pathé and Movietone newsreels and was shown in the tired housewife's slot in mid-afternoon. Crowned heads, bathing belles, railway smashes, fashion parades, dance marathons, boat launchings, hangings, the glossier phases of war – a poignant record of a vanished world; the world before information started to overwhelm experience. 'There is an excess of information, making us prisoners of the news.' This is the first thing young Ashley Cann ever said to me. 'It is as if history had caught up with us in the form of news. Don't you see? Yesterday's news becomes history, already just barely perceptible. It ages even more rapidly than fashion, of which it is an accelerated form.'

Just before Christmas I was summoned to an audience with the editor, a decent, shy, ferociously blushing Old Etonian, determined to play the white man. Due to my recent . . . ah . . . unfortunate history, and my . . . ah . . . how shall we . . . *breakdown*, from which he was assured I was well on my way to making a full and lasting recovery, I could no longer be risked on his . . . that is to say, the group's . . . flagship paper. However I was far too good a man to be let go. He had moved personally to ensure that I be given a berth on the sister, tabloid title. Which, after all, as he pointed out, was only the difference between taking the lift to the second floor rather than to the fourth. Saying which, he shook my hand, blushed a deeper crimson, and turned his attentions to a pot plant on his desk while his secretary showed me out.

They didn't exactly deck the halls with boughs of holly when I showed up at my new job on the first day. I was saddled with the household chores as I knew I would be, subbing letters and puzzles on the games page, checking facts, chasing down sources on the phone. But then I was saved by the General Election, which was called for May. At least it got me out into the world again, as a C-team sketch writer on the campaign trail.

It was like being back in Sunday school, taking charabanc trips and away-days around the country, with lucky-bags and fizzy drinks, being herded and coralled and counted on and off the bus to make sure that nobody was missing. And, barring an assassination attempt on the candidate or a major gaffe, there was nothing to file but bits of filler, waffling on the issues. (The editors didn't want scoops from us. All they wanted was to make sure that nobody else had got something that they didn't have. Sending them something nobody else had would have only thrown them for a loop and convinced them I was having a relapse.) It was the perfect convalescence, with no compunction to go round looking as if your dog has just run under a bus the way you have to when you're staking out the wife of a man who has been discovered keeping the body parts of children in a Wendy House in a lock-up garage, or when you're sitting round taking bets on what time on what day of the week a famous TV personality is going to die.

I have had relapses — panic flashbacks full of brain-jams and lacerating glass, followed by blackouts, numbness in the fingers of my right hand, palpitations, hallucinations; symptoms shared with the survivors of car-crashes, assaults, rapes, plane smashes, natural disasters and war. But by and large I keep my boat afloat with sleeping pills, sedatives, sputtering newsreels and films shot in black-and-white, and Meryl Streep's governessy tones. I feel simultaneously tangled up in and remote from events. There is a discrepancy between what I see and what I read about it the next morning, even when it is a report that carries my name. The more I do this, the more I wonder whether the things I've seen really are the things I've seen, or whether they are things I have merely read about or seen on television, and projected myself into later. I keep waiting for the night to descend the way it does in computer games – the sky goes out; it just suddenly goes dark.

Day 21. A question that's been bothering me since I woke up this morning (fully dressed, including battle-wearied Barbour and shoes) is: What did I have to eat last night? I know I had something and I have a reasonably vivid recollection of where I had it: a small, dark, Frenchified place, with amateurish waiters and the dry migrainous smell of new paint; there were pale pink and yellow flowers on the table, a wall hung with peasantware patterned plates, a brass jug on a hook by the door. It's what went into my mouth to blot up the cataract of Stolly's and other falling-down lotions that remains a blank.

All morning my stomach has been crying out for sustenance and my head has been asking to be put into some quiet, low-lighted space. And so, despite the high blood pressure, cardio-vascular problems and ever-present threat of palpitations; in the face of dire warnings about cholesterol levels and blood sugar, and the volatile cocktail of alcohol and antidepressants, here we are once more in the bottly light among the pebble-grain glass and the crusted tile mosaic and the brightwork, getting in the first of the day.

Although I am in a job that demands engagement and ingratiation, the glad hand, the lulling smile, and then peptic (ulcer-puncturing) forward propulsion, I find my instincts are all for retreat and withdrawal – to the dim nook, the worn leather, the brown shadows in the old corner. A backwards movement, a compulsive taking to cover, is one that feels engraved in my muscles. As a reflex it is never stronger than when I should be out there, as I should be now, on the loiter, attempting to intrude myself into the life of another stranger.

The cuts have been got together for me by Helen, and it's Helen's arms and hands I can see holding the gnarled clippings in place against the plate of the photocopier. For reasons of speed, I can only suppose, she has run them off without bothering to bring the lid down. The result is that, while I should be reading up the background on the story I'm supposed to be covering – a catalogue of slashings and shootings and other fleeting fish-wrap catastrophes – I find myself drawn instead to these spectral hands and arms which I am intrigued to find I am able to study in forensic detail, in all their cellular particulars. The high contrast throws into relief every grainy pore and follicle; every grooved cross-hatch and complex tonality; the way the fine dark hairs lap around the watch-strap; the triangle of moles below the wrist; the tapered fleshy cushions of the fingers, shot from below (the flash slicing along the wall) and spread flat against the glass.

Helen is not an attractive woman. No kind of sexual frisson, so far as I'm aware, has ever passed between us. And yet when I take her disembodied hand and place it near my lap, or lay her arm along my thigh, say – like this – I experience an unexpected but definite stirring.

A recurring element in all the cuts (one of the great pleasures of the job, after a story has been filed and a line drawn under it, is binning them) is maps whose inky arrows and star-flashes and blocks of filler Lettratone indicate that they are maps of places where news has suddenly erupted; where the comfortable façade of daily life has been torn away. But that was then.

It's now three years since Larry Brown, a policeman, was shot at point-blank range in a courtyard at the front of Orwell Court, a litter-strewn block of flats on the Suffolk Estate in Hackney. The man who ambushed and then killed him gave as his reason the fact that his girlfriend had dumped him the night before. He told detectives: 'I blew your copper away because my girl blew me away. I just did it. The first thing that came into my head was to kill a policeman.'

It's much longer – almost eighteen years – since another policeman, Stephen Tibble, was gunned down by an escaping IRA terrorist on a quiet street in Baron's Court in west London. He was shot twice in the chest and died two and a half hours later in hospital. (Helen's hand, looming out of the blackness, securing a picture of the dead policeman, captioned 'Victim', against the photocopier, has something of the aspect of a blackened hand gesturing from a shallow woodland grave within earshot of motorway traffic.)

Ronan McCloskey was on his fifth day of unsupervised duty as a policeman when he stopped and breathalysed a twenty-two-year-old man driving a Capri in Willesden High Road one night in May 1987. On the pretext of locking up the car, the man sped away with PC McCloskey trapped half in and half out of it. He drove at high speed for half a mile before crashing through a fence at the corner of Dudden Hill Lane and Denzil Road, NW10. Constable McCloskey was hurled against a concrete post and died of head injuries before he reached hospital.

Half the thirty-strong A-shift at Chelsea police station

77

were killed or wounded in the IRA bomb that went off in Hans Crescent, adjacent to Harrods, just before Christmas, 1983.

PC Keith Blakelock was hacked to death with knives and machetes during the Broadwater Farm riot in Tottenham in October 1985. (An attempt was made to hack off his head, with the intention of parading it on a pole.)

And at the sites of these and other police murders – Braybrook Street, Shepherd's Bush, W12; Montreal Place, off Aldwych, WC2; Higham Hill Road near the junction with Mayfield Road, Walthamstow, E17 – permanent memorials have been erected in recent years: small funerary monuments of Portland stone and granite and white-veined marble; important materials in unimportant, sometimes tawdry, settings; desolate reminders of solitary death in bright hospital rooms; of sudden death on the pavement.

Although there are people who bring them flowers, holly wreaths at Christmas, and small potted plants, there were always others who, even before the events of recent months, said the memorials were a source of negative energy which they claimed to have experienced as fields and waves of radiation and soft singing static. They believed there was something fetishistic or cultic about them (one woman told me the memorial close to where she lives had been put there to spy on her), and would cross the street in order not to have to pass too close to the bad ju-ju they were generating.

The first attack happened in April last year, in the vicinity of the stone erected in memory of PC McCloskey in Willesden: a young woman gagged and raped in some nearby bushes while walking home from a friend's house. The second rape took place in a mews at the rear of Harrods, and this time a knife was used. The rapist struck for the third and fourth times in Hackney and Tottenham, very close to where the officers Blakelock and Brown were killed.

The connection between the attacks and their locations remained speculative until the arrival of a set of pictures from the attacker whose existence has been withheld from the public but which I was given sight of thanks to a long-standing sweetheart deal between my paper and the police.

I turned up at the appointed time at the enquiry head-quarters and was shown into a cubicle room lined with battered file envelopes on industrial shelving and lighted by a huge rectangle window of wired glass. I was brought turbid brown tea in a mug with a faded Metropolitan Police badge on it — 'The Badge of Courage' the inscription read — and handed a buff folder by a detective sergeant whose 'Sick bastard' seemed as if it could apply to me as much as to the person in the smudges. It was a transaction loaded with these kinds of ambiguities, and I was aware of his physical closeness, of the close eye-balling he was giving me — on the look-out for some crotch action? any attempt to palm one of the slippery eight-by-tens? — as I undid the string-tie.

The penis in the pictures was that of (probably) a white male — the uncertainty was due to the fact that it was mottled, brown and pink; piebald like a horse. But the weird pigmentation was far from being the most distinctive feature: the shaft — and, in the later pictures, the glans — was pierced with bullet-headed silver studs, making it look notched, only semi-organic, and lending it the appearance of some kind of museumised medieval weaponry. The number of studs varied from picture to picture, but they didn't keep sequence with the attacks. They shone with the same value metal sheen as the gold in the declivities of the carved inscriptions of the stubby, phallus-shaped memorials against which they were carefully, semi-erectly posed.

This square is a favourite route for taxis going in to the West End from the south and west. There is a steady black stream, sluggish and black as oil, conduited along the northern side and off into the narrow channel to Regent Street, making the turn at the exact spot where WPC Yvonne Fletcher was mowed down, shot in the back, and killed.

The memorial that stands here, the first of the police memorials to go up in London, is white with a granite plaque bearing the standard inscription 'Here fell . . .', with the name and date. After ten years, the white of the stone is so very white it looks like a keyhole of light projected on to the railings and the tough green-black plants ranged behind it.

Because it is June, it is too early for the overhead trees to be slaked with dust and particles of carbon, but late enough for the young, lush leaves to throw a cooling shadow, trapping the air underneath. Even on the brightest day the white stone to Yvonne Fletcher has the fluctuating quality of light flickering at the back of a cave.

It has not been violated. It doesn't feature in the pictures. It is maintained in its pristine condition by a woman, a stranger unknown to Yvonne Fletcher at the time of her death, who makes regular expeditions from the small south-coast town where she lives to wash the stone and polish up the granite and set fresh flowers at the memorial's base.

It is an activity that she feels no compulsion to explain. Attempts were made to get her to sneeze it out in the first months after the memorial was unveiled, but she had made a commitment to remaining silent and wouldn't be budged.

And in the intervening years, so far as I know, she has been free to go about her janitoring undisturbed. But these are slow newsdays (Scott McGovern's death is still pending; the story will be stale buns soon). The coincidence of violent death and violent sex at the memorials is irresistible. It is a story that has to be kept at a rolling boil. Sebastian-Dominic dredged up a recollection of the woman at morning conference at the beginning of the week. A couple of calls to the budgie at the bill shop supplied likely days and times. And here I am, parked behind the cool, stone pillar of a shuttered building with an unobstructed view of the Yvonne Fletcher memorial, poised to invade its guardian's anonymity, ready to pounce.

I had anticipated that she would be approaching from Regent Street to the west, or Piccadilly to the north, which narrowed it down to three streets (and two pubs – the Tom-all-Alone's and The True Sun, from where I haven't long returned – a final *adiós* to the meltdown hangover with which I started the day, *buenos días* to tomorrow's). The route I hadn't counted on was along the gravel path of the formal garden in the centre of the square with its lunching office workers and lurid flower beds and central statue of William III.

But that's the way she must have come, because now all of a sudden she's there and already absorbed in her work: a medium-built, young-appearing middle-aged woman in trousers, a sweater and a rubberised anorak that she has taken off, folded and placed as padding under her knees. I know from sniffing around there that she keeps a container of water and a plastic atomiser wedged between the memorial and the metal fence; she has unpacked spray polishes and bleaches with emphatic labels and bright child-proof nozzles and a variety of other cleaning materials which are standing by waiting to be used.

Even before I break cover and take the first steps towards her, I have a vision of her life and a distinct image of a place I have never know. (Grids of lampposts, rows of urns and statues as points of identity and continuity in the vast space. The smell of real cakes through the doors and windows of the bakery.)

The whole of the south side of the square is undergoing renovation and all the buildings there have disappeared behind a false front – a simple-coloured, billboard-sized façade cartooning the eighteenth-century classical façades it conceals. Wide orange mesh covers the spaces of the windows, and men in safety helmets are visible there in such numbers that I feel like a show put on for their amusement as I emerge into this hot and intricately enclosed space. Through the path of the bullet that killed Yvonne Fletcher, through the accumulation of energies, past the place where her hat had lain, photographed but untouched, for many hours, a predator closing and closing on the unalerted woman on her knees.

It is an attitude that prompts a rush of images – darkly radiant, churchly lit images from pagan ritual and the scriptures. *Ecce ancilla Dei. Behold the handmaid of the Lord. The Madonna of Humility.* Hundreds of associations in a few seconds from far away.

But, at this point, three images predominantly: A man stepping round a woman who is on her knees with a brush and a bucket and abjectly imploring to be allowed to go where he is going. A woman looking up, blinking against the light that has just flooded the cupboard where she been forcibly shut away. A woman bent to the task of scouring a ring of dirt off a bath with the radio playing some hit from her youth in the morning after her husband has set out for the job both of them know in their blood he will soon be losing and the children have left for school. (No matter how strenuous our efforts to put a space between them and us, our own lives constantly invade us.)

There is a tin vase tethered by a chain to the railing at the side of the stone. Wisteria and lavender in a glass bottle. Primrose in pots placed in a tricolour basket. I'm almost there now, almost on the woman, but she still hasn't turned or given any sign that she knows that I'm approaching. It is as I am about to bring my hand in contact with the knotty open weave of her sweater, register the start of alarm, that I notice it has grown as quiet as cancer.

Amid all the noise of the city, there is an echo, an experience of quietness which is almost African in quality. 'Even,' I want to say. 'Even, stand up. Don't cry. Forgive me.' But it is barely dawn yet where Even is living, in a quiet subdivision near a lake. The woman glances back at me sleepily, trustingly, when she feels my hand on her neck and hears the sound of my wife's name.

T : H : R : E : E

Like many people of my age, I can remember as a boy squinting in through the window of the pub used most often by my parents – a popular local called The Duchess of Sunderland, in their case – trying to piece them together from the morselated images made by the ground and intricately engraved glass. I'd stand on the low sandstone window-sill with my eye close up against the refracting bulb of a thistle or the distorting leg of a fleur-de-lys, trying to locate them and piece them together in the promiscuous press of bodies in the bar. It is always winter, and there is always a fire whose fire colour divides and bleeds into the pattern incised into the window like molten metal running in troughs; and there is an excited hubbub in which I try to hear things that I'm not supposed to hear, but don't know what. I suppose I imagined forbidden things taking place in there: furtive gropings, banned substances being palmed, life-threatening infidelities – the dirty doings I read about weekly in the *News of the Screws* that they thought they had hidden out of harm's way, and that I guiltily tugged my todger to when I was sure I was at home on my own.

The world beyond the glass represented, from my child's perspective, a kind of deep-sea space in which they had the opportunity to immerse themselves – a luminous, beneficent, dense element – and in which I would immerse *myself*, when the time came. The barriered elsewhere of another world.

Since I came into my inheritance it is the pell-mell, work-aday world that has taken on a dreamy aspect, observed, as I so often observe it, from the bibulous, business side of the frosted glass. In the last few years a new rhythm – a pendulum pattern – has imposed itself on the frantic comings and goings of the daytime pavement traffic. Outside certain pubs at a certain time of the day now you will see men in suits ambulating backwards and forwards, metronomically up and down, talking into wafers of angled plastic and maintaining the even pace of the big-cat enclosure or the prison yard. They never trespass beyond the physical boundary of the pub, or stray more than a foot or two from the windows, and are as much a part of the street life as Simon-the-pieman or the rag-suited newsmonger or the little flower girl with her tray of violets were in days of yore. They have become a modern, lulling presence: dark, unfocused figures, between drinks, jawboning about product-flow and component com-patibility and profit centres, and intent on giving the impression that they are anywhere other than where they are, which is thirty seconds from the next chugalug (nobody is fooled). And always, in the background, the subliminal bloom of London's red buses, fogged below the advertising streamer, clear above it, like old-fashioned doctor's pick-me-ups, settled in the bottle.

The Cinq-Mars is one of many London pubs famous for its Dylan Thomas connection. There is nothing to commem-orate the fact that Dylan drank here (it is well off the tourist route). But it was the Dylan link that gave me the excuse to make it the kicking-off point on one of my first dates with Even.

Even was a striking, even eccentric, dresser in those days. She bought most of her clothes at street-markets or charity shops, and wore her hair plaited or coiled in braids around her ears. She wore jet necklaces, amber ear-rings, fishnet stockings, Utility dresses, plum-coloured lipstick and ankle socks. She smoked slim panatellas and could hold her drink. It was my idea to start off at The Cinq-Mars and spend the rest of the night doing a Dylan Thomas pub-crawl, in character, as Caitlin and Dylan. (We had fallen gratefully on the Thomases as a conversational gambit the first time we went out together. Even told me that Caitlin had been a dancer with the Tiller Girls at the Palladium, and later with the *Folies Bergère* in Paris, facts which I didn't know, and was pleased to learn.)

I wore a loud Viyella shirt and a Donegal-tweed tie for the occasion. Even turned up in a demob great-coat and a ratty fox fur with two road-rash heads and two pairs of tortured button eyes. She had a light ale and we stood at the crowded bar at The Cinq-Mars, which was a pub still popular then with the working man. 'The heavy scents of the masses,' I said, lacking all conviction, quoting I'm-not-sure-who, but not Dylan Thomas. 'With their disturbing messages of the intimate life.'

'Which March-the-fifth do you think it is?' Even asked after a while. 'The name of this pub,' she said, when it was clear I had no idea what she was talking about. Nobody who went there on a regular basis used the French pronunciation. Everybody always referred to it as The *Sink*-Mars, and it irritated me that she didn't know. I had always thought of the planet anyway, not the month. It had been a favourite watering-hole of Burgess and Maclean and their crowd in the early fifties, around the same time the Thomases were regulars. I considered telling Even this, but I involuntarily did something else instead. I lifted the flap on the pocket of the coat she was wearing, and tipped the two inches of beer sitting in my glass straight in. 'That wasn't supposed to happen yet,' she protested. 'We were supposed to build up to the bad behaviour part. The fisticuffs, the public spats. But' – here she took the fluff and sodden bus tickets and wet rubbish from her pocket and rammed it down my shirt – 'if that's how you want to play it, it's fine with me.'

We continued on to The Uncommercial Traveller (ice projectiles, Chinese burns, upsetting several other people's drinks), and then The Frozen Deep, where, both of us well on the way to being properly *in drink* now, the aggression took a serious turn. I got her in a half-Nelson until she begged to be let go; she ground a lighted panatella into the back of my hand, leaving an ash-rimmed glutinous crater. In a deserted garden square between The Frozen Deep and The Billy Bigelow we completed the process we had embarked on, and started hitting out at each other with an intention to really hurt. After a few minutes of this, Even took to her heels in the rain in tears, her foxes skinny and bedraggled, and I went and had another drink.

After the wedding (a quiet affair at Caxton Hall, although her father, the rag-worm and maggot millionaire, had pushed for a big production), we spent a week in a wooden bird-watchers' hut on a tidal marsh in Norfolk, reading by candle-light at night, watching the contents of the chemical toilet bobbing perkily outside the door in the mornings.

Even lost the taste for drink when she was pregnant with Tristan. She never went back to smoking after Jennifer was born. By the mid-seventies, in step with the magazines who employed her, she was experimenting with 'good' carbohydrate-based meals – cereals, wholegrain rice, lentils – and soya-based meat substitute. By 1978, when I moved out, she was a wild-eyed, carotin-coloured, card-carrying convert. She'd lie in bed at nights boning up on passive smoking and hydrogenated fats and retin-A, her corded neck, her rope-veined hands, her swarthy chest pulsing out their admonishments.

The house was full of yoghurt, filtered water, and people flossing. 'But Daddy you can't *eat* that,' Jennifer would wail when she saw me sitting down to my 'empty' calories (usually Frosties and a ketchup-topped bacon sandwich) in the mornings. I tried to explain that I *liked* the taste of diesel oil after it had been whipped up into a huge lump and pumped into doner kebabs and cheese slices and tangy snacks with flashes offering the chance to win a VW Golf Cabriolet and happy cartoon characters on their packets (my passport to the twiglet zone). Got actual pangs for the taste of Wonderloaf with its industrial yeast, treated flour, negative air and carcinogenically refined white sugar (unrivalled at soaking up the alcohol still sloshing round the system from the night before).

And I wasn't *just* being perverse. I knew the stuff I was cramming into my body was crap, but I also knew there was something seductive and pleasure-giving about it that had to do with resolving the distance you feel between the way you understand the external world and your emotional response to it. I was also convinced that in some ways it was a class issue (part of the reason I felt like a put-upon minority in my own home). Both my parents might have reamed out their systems with E-numbers and saturated fats and carbohydrates, but at least they didn't spend their last years

(I told Even) looking as if they'd just been given barbed-wire enemas. It seemed that the stringier Even had got, the more solemn she had become. 'Food's a very political area,' she'd explode at me. 'You don't seem to realise. Take a lot of cheap shit, make it look palatable and taste palatable, and people make fortunes. They have to keep selling this shit that people like you think is delicious to keep making money from it. There's not much money in selling a parsnip.'

'Do you know what you're turning into?' I'd snap back at her. 'You're turning into the sort of woman they seal the water glasses and toilet seats in hotels for. Mizz Crab-Apple, 1977.' And so on.

Even had a theory, from which she wouldn't be budged, that my breakdown was virtually one hundred per cent diet-related. And while she had me as a passive victim, I submitted to her regime of gin-seng and royal jelly and vitamin and mineral supplements. But, as I recovered, we reverted to our former positions, and bumped along, agreeing to disagree.

We had been separated for more than two years when Even met Glen Leithauser at some trade show or food industry convention, and within weeks (even now I'm hazy on the exact timetable – it might even have been within days) of meeting him decided to up-stumps and begin a completely new life in America. She took it as given that Tristan, then ten, and Jennifer, aged eight, would be going with her. I was in no position to argue, and in any case had always regarded myself as the big baby in the family; all three of them had always been there to pick up after and wipe and boost and coddle, to parent me. I loved them in a bred-in-the-bone, sentimental sense, but I didn't *know* them any more than I knew the people whose lives I crashed or greased my way into most weeks of the year, whatever I might have preferred to believe. I only listened when I was being paid to listen and had my antennae twitching for something that would stand up as a strong lead. During the rest of my existence I was on auto-pilot, part man, part machine: RoboHack.

Even organised a brief hello-and-goodbye dinner in a restaurant for the three of us – me, Glen Leithauser, and herself. (It was in fact the first and, so far, the only time I met the man under whose roof my children were to spend those all-important formative years.) I wish there was some gross indiscretion to own up to; I wish I could claim that something bloody-minded and eternally shaming occurred, some brainwarp or rush of blood to the head, a sociopathic lunge, an attempt to skewer Leithauser with the fish knife (on special occasions – of which this apparently counted as one – Leithauser allowed himself fish). In fact it was all as chummy as hell, and it was 'Glen' and 'Norman' almost before we'd been treated to a recital of the specials of the day.

Leithauser was a pioneer in the field of organically grown fruit and vegetables – peaches, red field tomatoes, tomatillos, eggplants, squash blossoms. Four years earlier he had been selling tomatoes from a garden he had cultivated in a place outside Buffalo to a few restaurants in up-state New York. By the time he met Even in 1981, he was piloting a twin-engined Cessna turboprop and enjoying a reputation as Mister Juicy Organic Tomato of the Eastern Seaboard states.

He was a collegiate lunk with fine brushcut hair and aviator glasses with an irritating luminescent lemon-yellow tint and a certain born-again something about him. He projected the righteous aura, the baritone coolness of the NASA space-age heroes of the sixties, when he would have been only slightly younger than Grissom, Glenn, Shepard and co. In his Shetland sweater and his khakis and his white, just-out-of-the-box New Balance tennis shoes, he could have come fresh from dunkin' a few balls in the basketball backboard attached to the garage of his ranch-style split-level. Even had had her hair cut in a new, neat asymmetrical style, shingled at the back, and the pair of them could have already been running for one of the cushier offices in the State.

For safety's sake, we kept the conversation on sap beetles and ground rot and the line in state-of-the-art, value-added organic gourmet dishes Leithauser was about to start selling into supermarkets all across America. I was able to chip in a few nuggets about Sam Walton, the founder of Wal-Mart and the then Richest Man in America, who I'd just read a profile of in a magazine.

'Oh yeah, great guy for in-the-trenches retailing and, above all, marketing. The man who revolutionised the show with down-home values,' Glen Leithauser said, quoting the article, so far as I remembered it, word for word. 'The guy who I'd really like to meet though is this guy,' he said, indicating the restaurant Muzak, which was then playing a Van Morrison track. 'I'd get really a heck of a kick out of going up to Van Morrison and addressing him by his real name, which is Ivan. *Ivan.* Can you believe that?'

'Oh Norman has met all kinds of celebrities,' Even said, with a look I had come to recognise over the years. To avert the next question, which is always Who is the most interesting person you have ever interviewed?, I jumped in and switched the conversation to the wine. It was a big thick bruiser of a Barolo, and I had it all to myself. They were drinking non-carbonated water without lemon. (A good-cop/bad-cop, third-degree interrogation of the waiter had eventually established that, yes, there was preservative wax on the lemon rind.)

Leithauser paid with the platinum card, then folded and filed the bill conscientiously away in his wallet. Some City boys, in striped shirts and felt braces, were having a boisterous time at another table, swigging champagne, skimming bread rolls at one another.

It was 1981, the summer of the riots. The summer my wife and children crated their belongings and moved out of my life. They have kept sporadically in touch. They send me pictures. Jennifer is studying mathematical physics at Boston University. Tristan graduated *summa cum laude* in merchandising, marketing and public relations arts and seems set to inherit what I'm sure he now regards as the family business. 'It's all about moving the merch off the shelves,' he wrote on the last postcard I got from him. On the front was a colour picture of one of the new store format A&Ps that cater to an upscale consumer base and which Tristan believes represent the future of niche-marketed premium organic perishables.

A while ago, a man slipped into the seat next to mine in The Cinq-Mars and tried to sell me the sorts of things my mother used to call dust-collectors – souvenirs whose fate was to be forgotten – at fifty pence apiece. He was wearing no socks, and had boiled-looking blistered feet and ankles piling over his plastic trainers. He smelled equally of stale sweat and a stale pungent aftershave. He'd rummage in the hold-all balanced on his knee and pull out one small, damaged and insignificant object after another – a cracked vase, a porcelain pig with an ear missing, a glass giraffe or bambi, some Smurf-esque creatures; then a rawhide dog bone, a dented can of aerosol lubricant, all of it obviously the portable booty of a house-clearance; the effects of somebody who had recently passed away. 'Fifty-pee,' he said. 'That's all. Fifty-pee. What's your problem?' I remained stony-faced. 'Okay. Tell you what. You can have the lot. How's that? The whole lot's yours for a fiver.' Eventually I took a small plaster basket with chipped plaster flowers clambering up the side just to get rid of him. It is sitting on the table in front of me now, looking like the little white cloud that cried. Inside it is a shrunken oasis of waxy green matter pierced by the stems of the dozens of flowers it must have once held. For an instant it reminded me of the fondant-like mass of the brain suspended in its jelly sac in the cranium, and of a quote garnered from a neuro-anatomist during my background researches into Scott McGovern: The brain secretes thought as the liver secretes bile. Brain tissue is not regenerative; once destroyed it is gone for ever.

There is a television over the bar. A few minutes ago the barmaid was watching an Australian soap about hospitals and doctors. That has been replaced by the quiz show that comes on every afternoon about this time and is taken as a signal by the stragglers that they should be making tracks back to their under-vented, miserly-partitioned stalls and cubicles.

This is wallpaper television and perfectly suited to the time of day. The set is to a formula: glitter graphics; columnated desks like piles of coins, with coloured lights that flash and flutter at punctuating moments and can give the appearance of being activated by the audience's applause, although this is pre-recorded. The contestants are the usual decruited business executives, stir-crazy housewives, pizza-faced forecourt attendants, and trainee sex offenders. The presenter is a recognisable daytime tellyperson – pulverisingly genial, bland as Philadelphia cream cheese.

'Well,' he's saying, 'it's a while since we've seen our first contestant, Steven, from Cheadle in Manchester. He's a laboratory technician and also interested in military history and Kipling. Is that fun, Steven? Kipling? I wouldn't know myself. I've never kippled.' (Canned laughter that rings poignantly around the now nearly empty bar.) 'I will start as we always do with a general knowledge question for one point. Finger on the buzzer. Here it is. The French designer whose aftershaves include Kouros and Jazz is Yves-who . . .?'

The only thing that lifts the show above the ordinary is the quiz-master's (they still call him this) route to the foothills of mini-stardom. Four years ago Sean Norwood was an estate agent in Croydon, in south London, with a wife, three children, and a nice home on a satellite development still in the final stages of completion. Then one morning he got up to find that Shane, the middle child and, at nine, the older of his two sons, was missing. An upper window had been forced, although Sean Norwood and his wife, asleep in the next room, had heard nothing. Part of a man's size-ten bootprint was found at the point where the partly made-up road leading to the house turned into gravelled slurry. But Shane's whereabouts have never been discovered.

I was at Glenwood Close (the neighbouring streets were Greenwood, Redwood and Laurelwood) by mid-morning, pitched into a situation as usual brimming with deadly negative potential. The estate was desolate in its newness and its evidence of status striving, wallet-strain and killer commutes. The whole thing could easily have whirled off the computer screens in the architect's office and planted itself on the hundred and fifty acres of reclaimed sheep meadow, spruce and with all graphic co-ordinates intact (seven floor-plans, twenty-one different exteriors, no identical models to be built next to or facing each other). The place felt as aberrant, foreign and hostile that November morning as the event that had been visited upon it.

So here we all were. I made a note of the 'Stranger danger' warning notices at the entrances to the ash- and ilex-bordered play areas, and the 'World Wildlife Fund' sticker on the window through which Shane Norwood's kidnapper had entered the house. Then I peeled away from the pack to go and find the abandoned mattress with its horse-hair stuffing and its continents of bodily stains which, invariably on these occasions, is never very far away.

I identified Sean Norwood's father, Stan, as a family member within minutes of going into the pub. In the same way that some blind people eventually acquire a touch so sensitive that they can identify playing cards by the infinitesimal thickness of the shapes printed on them, so my senses are honed to lock on to people caught up in victim stories.

I knew straightaway from his accent that Stan Norwood was from the same part of the world I am originally from. He had been a fitter in the shipyards and had migrated to the soft south in the fifties to claim some of its featherbededness for himself. (He had had a string of jobs, and a string of illnesses, including diphtheria, testicular cancer and shingles; he was currently working as a delivery man for the Cookie Coach Company, a job that required him to wear a 'Quality Street'-style cape-coat and squash hat and drive a vintage van with spoke-wheels and olde-worlde sign-writing on the side.)

I felt my own submerged accent returning and growing steadily thicker as we spoke, establishing a mutual link (so I hoped) with the old close communities of the north, and an age when things were repaired rather than jettisoned, junked, thrown away. (A time – this was the clear intimation – when children could sleep safely in their beds without the fear of being carried off by an evil stranger. A time when the four walls of a house seemed to offer secure protection against the secret intrusion of terror.) And yet even as we waxed nostalgic about the rag shop and the old feed store and other local landmarks that had long ago been reduced to rubble and bulldozed under, I kept itchily turning over the configuration of the name – Stan – Sean – Shane – and wondering whether it represented some mutation or progression, rushing headlong towards this ineffable conclusion; the breaking of a line.

Stan – Sean – Shane. My feeling was that it was something that had happened unplanned and – even now, with the three names monotonously mantra-ed alongside each other in cold type (at first this caused chaos among the copy-takers) – went unheeded; that it signalled a cheery lack of introversion in the Norwood clan, passed down from generation to generation. I was impatient to fuzzle it up into some sort of angle, or present it in such a way that it suggested some pseudo-psychological insight that the competition hadn't got on to yet.

When the grandfather looked like he was about to start making preparations to leave, I pressed my advantage. This had all the makings of a whopper, after all; a major 'Hey, Doris' story (and so it was to prove). And I knew the drift of the notes that would have been being pushed through the letterbox at Glenwood Close all day (I had left one myself): 'Dear Mr and Mrs Norwood, This is obviously a difficult/emotional/tragic time for you. And if you'd like to tell your story to someone who'll treat it with sympathy and understanding, please give me a call on my portable. I'm outside the house now if you want to talk. Certainly we can offer you protection from all the other papers.' (The money bids would come later; I knew X from *The Star* was already out there toting £5000 in used twenties in a briefcase.)

I made my pitch to old Stan now, in person, as I helped him into his overcoat, in an accent that had become indistinguishable from his own. An hour later, to the fury of the rest of the pack kicking their heels on the pavement, I was indoors, eliciting the factoids of Shane Norwood's life, riffling through the pictures, pocket tape turning, making all the right noises, face like a well-kept grave.

A doctor had been in to sedate the mother, who was upstairs with a WPC stationed by the bed. A uniformed policeman was in the kitchen, fielding the calls from hoaxers that had already started to flood in, interspersed with crank calls from those who claimed to know the boy had been taken by aliens. In Shane's room, his bed had become a mound of flowers, cellophane-wrapped and with a business-card bearing a newspaper logo attached to each artful spray. Disturb the crinkled, expensive surface, and you could have expected to find sandy soil and smooth spade-shaped clods of mud, rather than the Arsenal duvet, the pattern of rocket ships and spinning ringed Saturns on the pillow.

The house, like the estate, was only partly finished. Some walls were newly rendered and bare; some parts of some floors remained uncovered; there were manufacturers' labels sticking to the undersides of lavatories and sinks.

The three of us – Stan Norwood, Sean Norwood and myself – got through the best part of two bottles of Lamb's Navy rum, and I left with some good tales. Better yet – I could already feel the sun of Howie Dosson's approbation on my back as I took possession – I left with the tape Sean had shot with his Sony Handy-cam on a cross-Channel ferry just a few weeks earlier, and from which we were able to grab some good-value stills of Shane playing with his brother and sister. (The cassette went straight into the editor's safe afterwards to keep it out of the maulers of our rivals. Tosser played for time with the Norwoods by bulling them that it had gone missing 'at the printers' and bunged them a cheque for £500 as a temporary sweetener.)

Sean Norwood, it turned out, was a TV natural. He had obviously been a bit of a ducker-and-diver in his time (although he didn't have a record – the other papers immediately checked this, hoping to run a spoiler); he instinctively mastered the difficult feat of being distraught-with-dignity; made repeated appeals for the return of his son in a way that played expertly, though not cloyingly, on the universal reflex of tears; he looked good, he had an unfakeable feel-good factor, and the camera loved him. (This was whispered excitedly by young women with clipboards clutched to their chests in production suites all over London: 'The camera loves him.')

Very soon he was a powerful media presence, a fixture not only of the news bulletins, but also of magazine programmes, documentaries, phone-ins and talk shows. He started a foundation which campaigned on the issue of abducted children, sought new legislation and better education on child safety. A number of name columnists hailed him for having turned adversity to advantage, transformed personal tragedy into something positive, and found in his own catastrophe a cause. Five months after Shane's disappearance, he moved out of the family home in Glenwood Close, and in with one of these columnists in her house in Acton. Within what seemed a very short time, she was penning a column on the impossibility of living with a severely traumatised male. Sean Norwood had already moved on to a researcher from Yorkshire Television by then and was living in Leeds, where he was reported to be drinking (and, some said, drugging) heavily.

Although several men have claimed to have killed Shane Norwood, his family have never found out for certain who, if anybody, did; the body has never been discovered. His father's personal odyssey since the abduction has been a gift for the news media. There have been a series of other, widely publicised romances, and several public brawls. At one point Sean Norwood was rumoured to be hanging out in Dublin with Alex Higgins, Jerry Lee Lewis and some of the members of U2. There was the gun incident, following hard on the heels of the knife incident; and then, just over a year ago, he went into somewhere called the Exodus Recovery Centre in the West Country to dry out.

He emerged to tell the harrowing tale on the same shows on which he had originally appeared, three years earlier, to talk about Shane. Soon there was the autobiography, which is still in the upper reaches of the best-sellers after five months, kept there by his new-found popularity as an afternoon quiz-show host.

I am looking at Sean now, playing to an audience of three through the sidewardly spiralling dust motes in The Cinq-Mars. He has just asked a woman called Esme, who is already taking home a computer chess game and a Kenwood cordless kettle, which sex symbol's original name was Norma Jean Baker, and Esme has given the correct answer, which is Marilyn Monroe. 'Marilyn Monroe!' he says, as if she had just recited Otto Hahn's third law of thermoneutics and nuclear fission. 'If you'd been given that name, you'd have changed it too, wouldn't you Esme?'

Sean Norwood's face glows throughout its 625 lines with sincerity, humility, vigour, and a creamy resonance – no sign of human hurtability there. But whenever I look at this face, I see the counter-image – the face I saw on the night his son disappeared, as we sat passing the bottle of syrupy rum: a face transformed by the ecstasy of pain, the rapture of grief; scalded by tears, smeared with phlegm and giesers of green snot. It is the sort of moment phots like Heath Hawkins see it as their life's calling to capture: human features calamitised by pain or terror; the moment of absolute animal abandonment.

The theme music is being brought up gradually now, and Sean Norwood is doing what he does at the wind-up of every show. 'Say "Goodbye, Shane," ' he says to the contestants, who, familiar with the format, are already waving in unison at the portrait of Shane Norwood which dominates a corner of the set that has been kept in darkness until now – a big blown-up innocent picture – the picture of innocence – surrounded by the hokey glamour of several dozen twinkling pearloid bulbs.

The makers of the show have not plumped for the sharp, professionally posed portrait that was available, showing Shane smiling and well groomed. They have opted instead for a snapshot picture – a second-generation print enlarged from copy negatives and pushed until it has a crude, documentary feel at odds with its showbizzy setting. Because of its lack of definition and precision, it seems irradiated with muted pathos; glutted with event-value.

'Bye, Shane,' Sean Norwood says, when the contestants

have finished waving their goodbyes. And then, turning to camera: 'Bye, everybody. And remember – be good, and if you can't be good, be careful. S'long. See you next time.' Cue credits.

'Bye, Shane,' a voice calls from across the bar. It's the man who sold me the plaster dust-collector, still sitting with his lopsided bag of junk on his knee.

An ambulance is travelling in our direction with its two-noted siren sounding. 'There's my taxi,' the man says, but he doesn't move.

My landlady, Mrs Norstrom, is an engaging old bigot who spends her days in her housecoat and her vivid russet wig lighting up and coughing into the phone and watching television at her kitchen table. She used to run the place as a rooming-house in the fifties, and a sign that used to hang in the street window then – 'No Irish, No coloureds, No dogs' – dangles from a coat-hook in the kitchen now, so that these two antiques (of sentimental value only) are often what you see (if you can see through the condensation and the spuming cigarette smoke and the low-lying clouds of fry-up fug) when you open the front door into the spartan hall.

I was aware in the early years of my tenancy, when she could still make the stairs, that she used to go and grub about in my flat when I wasn't there. I knew, but, because it fed into some romantic Greeneian notion of the aromatic genteel squalor of Earls Court doss-downs and Kilburn bed-sits (a notion that the wheezing crumblies and crones who were my fellow tenants did nothing to contradict and was, if anything, reinforced as the yuppy eighties got under way), I didn't care. There was less alienation involved in this new life than in Saturday-night come-casual supper parties and balls-aching conversations about extra-virgin cold-press olive oil and the human catastrophe of Somalia and the school-run – the life I had left behind.

What was she going to find up there in any case, other than the odd incriminating bottle or tumbler on the edge of the bathroom sink (I sometimes still like to start the day with fizzy vitamins or Alka-Seltzer beefed up with a four-finger splash of vodka), the odd stroke book spreadeagled on the floor, cockeyed piles of plates crusting over, and other common-or-garden evidence of the married bachelor life? Like Fowler, the Vietnam-based hack in Greene's *The Quiet American*, I was finally not involved. Not involved. Let them fight, let them love, let them murder, I would not be involved. 'I wrote what I saw: I took no action – even an opinion is a kind of action.'

Apart from Even and Tristan and Jennifer, and Therese 'Gumshoe' Norstrom, I can count the number of people who have been in here on the fingers of one hand and still hold a hamburger. I am that peculiar specimen that this odd profession produces by the containerload: the cocooned mixer; the gregarious loner.

If – when (oh and I'm increasingly inclined to think of it as when) – the fetid odour leaking into the common parts via the draught space at the bottom (and the top, and the sides) of my door results in the alarm being raised and the emergency services being called – Mrs N gawping up the stairwell, hair evenly quilted into squares of baldness by her curlers, dressing-gown clutched modestly at her throat; the rest of the inmates hanging out of their doors in their thermal underpants and crochet shawls and thick, pilled night apparel, the nails of their aged toes clicking like beaks against the chill old-as-the-century tiles, players in an award-winning, promenade production of the *Marat/Sade* – if/when the time comes for outside agents to break their way into the Greeneland of my humble, down-at-heel accommodation, you can bet the farm that they will home in on the one item flagging its oddness and incongruity, convinced that here they have stumbled across the key which will unlock the sickness of my soul, throw a revealing beam through the murkiness of my parasitical, sadsack personality.

High on my pillow, standing sentry over my blackened, worm-meat remains, will be the companion of my declining years, my confidant, my china, my (if you insist – and, let's face it, you will insist, liking the sound, the inference, the suggestion of some strange intimacy, the subtle but palpable eroticism) – my fetish.

Physically, my polyester-wadded friend will by then be in the same desperate shape as myself – dust, light, damp and pests (the larvae of the carpet beetle, the spore of the clothes moth) taking their toll of his pastel nylon pelt; the stuffing of polystyrene pellet mix and low-grade synthetic waste trickling out of the open leg- and body-seams; the raised script of the label sewn into the seam-edging of the half-wasted, half-elephantiasised foot – *Fullalove* – made illegible by coffee, wine, egg, soy sauce, ketchup and other tricky-to-deal-with stains. He will be looking, that is to say, as he would have looked if he had ever reached his intended destination all those years ago and been made to take his chances in the world.

'Hello, pally' or 'So pal, what can I tell you?' or 'Any messages?' or 'Well pal, what's new?' Words addressed to a two-foot-long by foot-and-a-half-high, orange-and-yellow plush, saucer-eyed Everypup, sitting obediently where I placed him many hours earlier, patiently awaiting my return.

The head is a big head – bigger than it should be for the body, like a baby's – and the street lights throw its shadow many times bigger than lifesize across the unlighted room. My room has the look of a child's room in these (invariably inebriated) moments – an unimpeachable, safe place – and never fails to strike me as a place I want to be.

There's a joke that runs round what I suppose we have still got to call Fleet Street every time a story breaks that is big enough to have Tosser Dosson and his competitors slapping their cheque-books on the table. The *Mail/Express/Today/Sun/Mirror* might have got alongside the wife/daughter/mother/mistress (the joke goes), but 'Clit' Carson has got *inside* the wife/daughter/all of the above.

In another era, Robin Carson would probably have been a snatch-man – an operator whose job was to acquire pictures of people who were no longer in a position to be photographed (murder victims, people who had died in some disaster or other) from people who, for obvious reasons, were usually reluctant to part with them. A common tactic, once the snatch-man had weaselled his way into the house, was to suggest to the distraught mother/other that she nip into the kitchen and make a cup of tea. While she was gone he would strip the walls, sideboard and mantelpiece of every picture he could lay his hands on, and leg it before she reappeared. When they had been copied, he (sometimes) just pushed them through the letterbox.

But different folks – the baby-butchers and child flayers, the gerontomonsters and paedobeasts, the blood-satanists, human goulashers and media-wise thrill killers who make today's running – demand different strokes. And Robin 'Clit'

Carson, the best-known unknown star in the Fleet Street firmament, has risen triumphantly to seize the moment.

'In like Flynn' is the expression often used about Carson by the older managerial suits, men among whom the phrase 'the four-F Club' – 'Find 'em, feel 'em, fuck 'em, forget 'em – still has some currency if not a great deal of personal relevance. Carson's skills as a cocksman have earned him a Saab 900 convertible, a serviced flat in Kensington and the dubious privilege of charvering the female family members of some of the most notorious sickos and psychopaths of recent years (and/or, not unusually, the female family members of some of their victims). The primary objective is the same as it ever was: to relieve them of all visual material in every medium for a minimal outlay. Once that has been achieved, the secondary objective is to take them out of circulation so that the competition can't try to box them off or get them to do a turn without you knowing. The country house hotel (room fax, cable television, sauna, squash, Michelin-starred restaurant, forest- or lake-views optional) is ideally suited to this purpose, and has the added advantage of militating for the desired interviewer–interviewee legover situation. (Or 'The opportunity of assuring her that she is not alone, engulfed, in her adversity', as Clit would undoubtedly put it.)

Although doing a kindness to the women connected by blood, marriage or happenstance to notorious atrocity cases is a non-job filled by an un-person – it won't show up in the records; there is nothing on paper: 'editorial consultant' is Robin Carson's official job description – he has established himself as a property now worth well into six figures in the transfer market. (He has been turning out for our team for two and a half years, although there are currently rumours of an attempt – I've heard £125K mentioned purely as a sign-on – to lure him away.)

If the picture you're beginning to piece together from this is of somebody who thinks he's the first piece of white bread to come wrapped in plastic, then you're not much mistaken. Apart from his natural endowment – and of course there is endless edgy speculation about exactly *how* big, as well as endless playtime jokes about writing *to length* and making stories *stand up* and letting the subs have an extra nine inches – he is the owner of a body that has been remorselessly built up and stripped down, toned and tuned and lathed, stretched and finessed until it is performance perfect.

Naturally he jogs, and never fails to cause consternation when he squeezes into the lift after lunch with sweat streaming over his deltoids and pecs and dock-rope-like sternocleidomastoid muscles. Several times a week there are re-runs of the scene in *A Streetcar Named Desire* when Marlon Brando swaggers into the house and peels off his T-shirt ('Hey, you mind I make myself comfortable? My shirt is sticking on me') and Vivien Leigh as Blanche Du Bois, taking in his abdominal obliques and the cleated forearms with the raised basilic veins, dissolves in embarrassment and confusion. There are men too – I'm sometimes one of them – who choose the fire-stairs or the atriumed front entrance rather than risk a crushing, scrotum-tightening, close-quarters confrontation.

Carson is thirty-two or -three, blond and (except when he is out earning his keep, when he wears easy-to-spot, big-name logos and strafing Big Lunch ties) studiedly understated in his appearance. 'I think how people dress' – I promise I have heard him say this – 'is a function of where they are in the search for their bodies.' He goes in for loose unstructured jackets with exposed surface seams; expensively simple shirts made out of Sea Island cotton and Thai silk; flapping macs, stout outdoorsman shoes and designer document-cases and backpacks. At a guess, you would say he was in advertising or poetry, or a popular form-master in a fashionable prep school. (Carson claims to have gone to one of the minor public schools, but is so up-rooted and free-floating, part of nothing, adrift from any sense of a conventional code or tradition; value-free, morally chaotic – that this, like so much else of the Gatsby-esque about him, has to be uninspired invention.) His one distinguishing feature – although Clit himself obviously regards it as his single serious disfigurement – is the strawberry birthmark that pokes out of his shirt and laps round the lobe of his left ear like a burning admission of the covert relationship he enjoys with the dirty devices of the world.

So far, I suppose, so fairly predictable. What is less predictable is how he goes about getting a result in situations that, at a first glance, don't exactly seem charged with erotic possibility. The key is to ignore the big picture – the testosterone-charged galoot with the schoolboy-parted hair, still labouring under the illusion of eternal health and strength – and concentrate for a second on his face. What you see is not the chronic vivacity peculiar to the piranhas of the smiling professions, nor the vaporous mask of plausibility and ingratiation corona-ed with creeping guilt; what you see with Clit is something infinitely more sinister – the inward, doped-over look of the meditator or chanter, the socio-therapeutic New Ager; the 'enabler' he sells himself as being.

Carson has run the gamut of gurus and consciousness crazes: TA, TM, EST, Arica, rolfing, transpersonal psychology, yoga. And, if nothing else, one thing they have taught him is a way of making himself heard through the cyclone of psychic noise that sweeps in round the household of the latest basher-and-slasher or serial killer. The pleas and bullyings and hastily drafted licences and contracts fisted through the door by other journos are part of the frenzy – part of the carnival jabber and babble; Robin Carson's overtures, on the other hand, set out to get noticed by being like a whisper or a ululation.

He makes his initial approach via a message written in crowded copperplate on the back of a picture postcard with overt mystical or inspirational content, usually reflecting his latest spiritual enthusiasm. In the period that we have been casually yoked together as a team, these have included pictures of the Seven Pagodas, the shrines on the seashore at Mahabalipuram, Madras; the Temple of the Emerald Buddha, Bangkok; and portraits of Sri Chinmoy, Meher Baba, the Dalai Lama, and a pouch-cheeked Mongolian monk brought to public notice by one of the younger Royals and the owner of the Body Shop, who then had just established an ashram in Bourton on the Water in the Cotswolds.

Carson briefly sets out his stall – 'I'm emotionally available. I'm willing to go into the darkness with people. I hear the fear and am willing to go with them where it hurts' and so on; lists some of his greatest past successes – X, the Lust Killer, Y, the Motorway Monster, Z, Manchester's Baby-faced Serial Sex Murderer; and ends with a quotation from the Scriptures or a Sufi proverb or Zen koan.

Two years ago, Robin Carson was in the honeymoon period of his infatuation with the American beatnik-turned-Trappist visionary, Thomas Merton. He went about with postcards of the giant reclining Buddhas of Polonnaruwa in Ceylon, which Merton had visited a few days before his death; also a paperback book containing Merton's collected wit and wisdom which I suspected at the most Clit had only ever dipped into, but had gone over key passages in pink or yellow to give the impression of a close reading. ('What is important is not liberation from the body but liberation from the mind. We are not entangled in our own body but entangled in our own mind.')

It was with these weapons that Carson set out to get into the pants of the wife of a man whose crimes had been excitingly dire enough to be given maximum play on television and in the papers over the previous year and a half.

George Arthur ('Joe') Stires was the manager of a small refrigerated warehouse in Keighley, in West Yorkshire, that was used for storing live shellfish – crayfish, langoustines, oysters mainly from the west of Ireland, which went into large glass-fronted, oxygenated tanks. The cargoes arrived and departed at odd hours, and Stires had to be there to unlock the gates to let the drivers in and out. He had an old ottoman bed in a storeroom on the premises, where he lolled or lolloped like some great marine beast, some barnacle-backed crab or jelloid bottom-feeder. He whiled away the hours reading – he had a collection of books on judo, karate, palmistry, hypnotism, devilry, torture and Gilles de Rais, the Black Baron – and filing bits of scrap metal down into tiny needle-and scalpel-like knives, some of which he part-wrapped with strips of white cloth, which gave them the look of bandaged limbs or miniature, swaddled corpses; the others he inserted into two rag bands which, it was discovered when he was arrested, he wore tied lethally around his wrists.

Stires targeted as his victims young girls with ponies. The first two children suffered mysterious punctures and lacerations, but they – and their horses – survived the attacks. The third time he struck, though, Stires achieved what he had set out to do: girl and pony were both found dead in a field, with the pony's cooling, milky-blue entrails coiled intricately around the girl's neck. There were two more attempted murders, and two more actual murders conforming to the pattern of the first. Stires was arrested on his way home from the scene of the final killing, when police in a patrol car spotted him jumping a set of red lights and gave chase.

First question: Did Rachel Stires, who worked as a part-time lollipop lady in the nearest village, know she had been married to a monster? First priority: pictures – wedding pictures, holiday pictures, childhood pictures, any pictures. A job for the cavalry. Get Robin Carson up there – *like, yesterday* – to hit her with his bullshit ('He does a lot of shitting but his pants aren't down,' I happen to know is Tosser's private opinion) and give her a yea good – *yea good!* – seeing to.

In the immediate aftermath of the news that the caring koi-carp rearer and dog-walker, the motorbike tinkerer and Gloria Hunniford devotee with whom they shared their lives was also a masked rapist and dismemberer of little girls, a strange tranquillity, a kind of bliss even, often descends on women like Rachel Stires, as if the body was pumping out its own opiates or fogging narcotics and analgesics. It can take a week or longer (sometimes it never happens) for the anguish and self-chastisement to kick in, and for the low operatics of the TV miniseries and dramadoc to manifest itself. When he can get this to happen, Robin Carson knows he is getting close to hitting pay dirt, and to check-out time.

Having extracted the subject from her home environment,

with all its associations of familiar objects turned baleful and sinister, he commences the softening-up process the cult religions call love-bombing and Clit himself calls 'TLC' ('tender loving care'). The consoling squeeze of the hand, the gentle stroke of the hair, the brushing of lips against forehead, the nuzzling of the ear . . . What started as a career-opening has mutated into an aberrant, highly esoteric turn-on. Carson has become addicted to the taste (he told me this; he tells everybody this; he dines out on the story) of licked-up salt snot and hot grief mucus and nectared/saline tears. He has become convinced the taste is hormonal, its aphrodisiac tang the result of some chemical released into the body – the morphising agent, perhaps – at times of soul-crunching suffering and trauma. If you could bottle it, he is fond of saying, it would make somebody rich many times over.

Carson is a narcissist, numb with self-love. We have all grown skins, performance membranes, insulating layers; a dense wall of *lontananza* between ourselves and the world. But Clit is desensitised to a degree that makes the rest of us look like the Little Sisters of Perpetual Sorrow. He is icily detached, deficient in genuine feelings of sadness. He inflicts a rehearsed, facetious kindness in the same way that a torturer inflicts physical pain to get his victims to open up. And I am his collaborator; his accomplice in most regards. So what does that make me? Carson works the women over, coaxes them into a state of emotional free-fall, brings them on-side; but his talents end there. It is up to me to go in and point up the details of the broadbrush picture he will have provided, and package the out-pourings into some merchandisable form: 'The meat's on the hook, the money's on the table.'

It took the plods forty-eight hours of intensive questioning to satisfy themselves that Rachel Stires wasn't implicated in her husband's crimes. When they were sure, they installed her in the nurses' hostel they had nominated as a safe house, where she lived in terror of being sniffed out by people exactly like us.

It was hard to get near the Stires story. Everything was shut off. But through the girl on the till at the local '8–Til-Late' who he was using to take his messages for him (it is never safe to have messages left at the hotel), Clit was introduced to somebody who knew somebody who knew where Stires's wife was being mothballed.

He hand-delivered the postcard of the giant reclining Buddhas of Polonnaruwa containing his usual snow-job to the nurses' hostel on a Tuesday ('You have to live your recovery. You are the programme'). By lunchtime on Thursday, Clit and Rachel Stires were checking in under assumed names at the creeper-clad country hotel in Cumbria with the springer spaniels (mother and daughter) asleep on the steps and conical bay trees flanking the entrance and embossed matchbooks and Imperial mints and pot-pourri in venerable chipped bowls at Reception. It was the first of the five interchangeable establishments they checked into in the course of a week, always staying just one step ahead of the pack, who were in pursuit; and Rachel went on looking like a foundling, a member of the tragic army of the dispossessed, in all of them: uncomfortable with the menus and the deference and the carpeting (she had no carpets at home, except the narrow strip running in front of the sofa in the living room), she kept stealing away to have a brew-up with the pot-washers in the kitchen, or grabbing a duster and an apron and helping the chambermaids service the rooms.

Back at the terraced cottage that she had moved into on the day she was married, she let Clit clean her out of snaps of herself and the 'Gymkana Monster' (Ronnie Duncan still claims the credit for this); he left with plastic wallets, laminated folders, a perspex cube that had stood on top of the television, hand-decorated albums. The heat had been taken off the house by then – there were a few stringers and agency cowboys lurking about – and I spent a couple of days taking down the 'My life with . . .' material that would be the selling point of the eighteen-page, through-colour, pull-out section that we were going to get on the streets within hours of Joe Stires being sent down.

Rachel Stires was pleasant-looking in a skinny, country nutty, windburned lollypop-lady sort of way. She had her hair pulled back in a heavy pony-tail, and wore velour track suits and plastic flower-shaped ear-rings of the kind people used to throw darts and shoot down ping-pong balls to win at travelling fairs. I brought bottles of Blue Nun to the sessions, and she prepared trim triangular sandwiches garnished with potato crisps and cress and served with quality-weight paper napkins saved from one or another of the hotels where they had stayed. She had collected the matchbooks together in a soup bowl on the low table, where there was also a bowl of sharp-smelling pot-pourri with the satin bow from the original packet adrift in the middle of it.

There were some tears, not many (Clit had drunk deep), as I led her through the high- and low-lights of her, on the face it, not very eventful life, year by bald year, from the cradle to the Old Bailey, all the time of course hoping to draw out of her the authenticating details that would convince (a) Howie Dosson, and (b) the readers that they were getting the hot poop, and that she would divulge it to nobody else. (Joe Stires, ten years her senior, had set his wife on a pedestal, said he considered her a goddess. 'When I married you, I reached for a star and a farmhorse like me could never keep up with a thoroughbred like you,' he wrote to her from prison. He had a fetish about washing himself in Dettol and had been impotent for most of their married life.)

At the end of the second session, she posed for a picture perched on the greasy arm of what had been her husband's favourite chair. While the photographer was getting her to lower her chin, move her knee to the left a little, moisten her lips, I noticed for the first time that her wedding ring was missing from her left hand, although her fingernails retained their opaque rainbow shimmer. So when he'd got his snap, I switched the machine back on for a few more minutes and we covered that.

It was as we were preparing to leave that she reached down behind the sofa without moving from where she was sitting and produced the tilt-headed cuddly toy which she asked us to place on the impromptu memorial to Roxanne Boothe, the last of her husband's victims, something she didn't feel able to do herself; the shrine was along a part of the rusticated fence surrounding the field where he had surprised the girl feeding her pony, and we had to pass it en route to the motorway and the long drive south.

We took a wrong turn four or five miles out of the village, and passed the same barn three times from different directions before finding ourselves suddenly merging right with the early evening traffic onto a sliproad of the M66. We rode in silence for some time, zipping down the fast lane, bullying the reps and snowy-shouldered middle-managers out of our way, feeling righteous, adrenalised, bringing home the bacon.

It wasn't until we pulled into the services that we saw the nylon-plush puppy sitting at a tipsy angle on top of the blanket thrown over the photographer's tripods and titanium carrying cases to shield them from prying eyes. The blank, generic face inside the heat-sealed factory wrapping seemed to belong to this no-place of machine-vended convenience snacks and strategically racked impulse buys and urgent fluorescent colours; contiguous with the high-gloss, the pristine finish, the charged over-lit spaces. Cloned members of its tribe or batch were almost certainly on sale inside the beckoning, islanded glass box, waiting to do duty as comforters to choleric, fractious children on monotonous motorway journeys. It was impassive, inviolate; prescriptively winsome until moving lights, washing over the clear plastic wrap, fleetingly scrambled, unprettified, the features.

When we were back in London, the photographer made a detour to drop me off where I live. 'Don't forget this,' he called after me after I had slammed the door closed (a light went on in a window of the house opposite). He groped behind him in the dark, just the way Rachel Stires had done five hours earlier, and held the puppy aloft in his right hand above the roof of the car. I could have walked around into the road to get it, but instead I pressed myself against the near-side window and reached across the frosting metal until, as I now imagine it, I must have looked like somebody stretching for something that seemed in imminent danger of being snatched away.

The cold of the street after the heat of the car had misted the inner surface of the bag – misted and moistened it like a microclimate of exhaled breath. It was as if there was something alive in there – some undefined yellow-orange thing, fat and plush – struggling to breathe. (Who wrote that our lives begin with a slither through a tight place and end with being pushed deeper and deeper into a black sack?) There was a card cheaply printed with a picture of bluebirds trailing satin ribbons taped to the cellophane protecting the dog. 'A sweet little rose, loaned not given/To bud on earth and now blooming in heaven – I'm sorry. Condoalenses. R. Stires (Mrs)', it said in fading blue biro.

'I hope you'll be very happy together,' the photographer shouted as he sped away.

> The Skin Horse had lived longer in the nursery than any
> of the others. He was so old that his brown coat was
> bald in patches and showed the seams underneath, and
> most of the hairs in his tail had been pulled out to string
> bead necklaces. He was wise, for he had seen a long
> succession of mechanical toys arrive to boast and swagger,
> and by-and-by break their mainsprings and pass away,
> and he knew they were only toys, and would never turn
> into anything else. For nursery magic is very strange and
> wonderful, and only those playthings that are old and
> wise and experienced like the Skin Horse understand all
> about it.

Reporting is a perversion of normal existence, Even was forever telling me. 'You get to know them so that they feel relaxed with you, ask them questions you have no natural right to expect answers to, ask to see things you weren't meant to see, they open a window on the most intimate parts of their lives, and then you walk away.'

Walk, run, hop it, skedaddle. Sometimes empty-handed, sometimes not. The world rushes on, the urgency is redirected, the appetite for catastrophe finds a new focus. And as the tide recedes, it leaves in its wake the material evidence. Without intending to I have put together a yellow

museum of my infidelities, hollow promises, rank opportun-
ism, cowardice and bad faith.

'History in a hurry'. This is the definition of journalism
that those of us up to our necks in it in the trenches tend to
cleave to. 'Hot history'. It offers the promise of permanence
to something we know is written on the wind; it gives a gloss
of respectability to what is often no more than meddlesome-
ness; it sanctions the thrust forward to the next front, with no
thought for the casualties we are leaving behind.

To enumerate every item in my inglorious collection –
letters unopened, unacknowledged and unread; pleas for help
or information ignored; keepsakes unreturned; pictures cropped or otherwise mutilated beyond recognition, all of it
dating back a dozen years – would take too long and would
take self-laceration to the kind of lengths to which I am not
prepared to go. But as a bore-sample of my crapitude and
indigence, chew on these:

– the videotape of the star boy footballer who lay down on
a railway line after being dropped from the England under-
15 team for an important home international, entrusted to
me by his parents
– the minicassette containing the last message left by their
daughter on her parents' answer machine before she, along
with her husband and three children, was blasted out of the
sky five miles over Lockerbie
– a letter which ends 'I do appreciate there is no reason on
earth why you should in any way help me, but human
understanding is a thing I still have great faith in' whose
substance I can't bring myself to explore
– a soapstone ring given to me by a girl fan outside a hotel,
which I was supposed to pass on to David Bowie

– a request (ignored) from a woman wanting to be put in touch with the old school friend she hadn't seen for twenty-five years, whose daughter had just become the thirteenth victim of the Yorkshire Ripper.

To this rancid pile, add the little dog whose fate should have been to end up in a farmer's field outside Keighley in West Yorkshire, and then maybe as a mascot wired to the radiator grille of the refuse truck given the task, after a respectable interval, of clearing the memorial away.

For two years the little dog lay ignored in a corner, slowly disappearing behind the layers of dust and the yellowing cellophane. He became a fixture. I didn't see him. I soon forgot he was there. For the story of how he was finally sprung from this limbo-life to become my *gris-gris* or *nkisi*, my spirit-catcher, my boon companion and talisman, we have to go back more than a year.

I had been to a leaving-party – the latest in a long line of leaving-parties for men my age and younger who had out-stayed their welcome and were scrapheap-bound. The party started in the upper room of an old haunt in Fetter Lane called The Tickle Pink, and moved on in due course to the Press Club. Around four in the morning, the die-hards (Myc Doohan, briefly off the wagon, myself and three or four others similarly placed) were heading for some dump in the Mile End/Stratford area run by the son-in-law or father-in-law or brother of somebody (we were all too crocked to remember who) travelling in the cab in front.

We had stopped at a set of traffic lights in Queen Victoria Street in the City when the front of the taxi was lifted clear of the ground by the deep whump! of what, even where we were orbiting, we all knew straightaway was a bomb. The taxi windows, and the windows of the shadowed, institutional buildings closest to us, remained intact. But after a dangling moment of anticipation and terror, a blind hover in time, the cupric and opal and mercurichrome skins of the high-rises above and beyond us tightened and then bellied and ruptured to gorgeous and catastrophic effect: out of the vapours and dusts emerged stacks of brilliantly variegated tatters, like a finale at the autumn catwalk shows; like flesh hanging off a kipper bone. Before we had a chance to get our fists up to our faces to unpop our ears, the driver had locked into a U-ie, and was flooring the cab away from the danger zone.

Whoa! Hey! Where-the! What-the! Whooooa! Stop! We fell over each other trying to get at the sliding glass panel behind his colour-drained head. We were sitting on top of a story. Here was a chance to delay our own evenings of mutilated Stiltons and sad vol-au-vents and sozzled speeches and dusty boards (and the shed-sitting, wood-whit-tling, golf-playing, post office-queuing years ahead). We skipped like five-year-olds towards the already paling pall of smoke, beautiful against a murky orange dawn, the declara-tive sentences and stubby paras forming by force of habit in our pounding thick heads.

The body-count wasn't high (only one fatality, several lacerations, one serious). But there were important political implications and I was able to phone through some not-half-bad colour copy (paling pall, tragic tequila dawn), along with some eye-witness quotes, which made it into the late London editions.

By then the adrenalin and the need to get a grip had burned off some of the alcoholic haze. I was at that dangerous stage where the edge put on the night before was beginning to give way to the thud of blood at the base of the skull, and the shakes; birds were singing, and reality was beginning to intrude. With Myc Doohan, I took a taxi to Smithfield market, where the pubs were serving breakfast and you could get a drink.

The hours that followed are something of a blank. I remember the first port and brandy, and maybe the one that followed that. I don't remember falling backwards off the stool while putting over a brief up-date on the scene at the devastation area as we had left it (Doohan apparently got to me in time to stop me cracking open my skull like a pumpkin, and finished dictating the remainder of what I was going to say without missing a beat). I have no recollection of the taxi ride to Seven Dials, or of being deposited in the room where I eventually, briefly, came to.

I do remember working out, with the utmost difficulty, what time of day and where I must be: it was just beginning to get dark, coming up to the Happy Hour, with lights from the traffic filtering through the mealy calico blind and slipping over the cockerel-green painted walls, the plaster-board filling the space where a door had recently been, the pasted-on dado line, and the poster of a smoke-wreathed, curly-headed man I recognised as Lenny Bruce.

I was lying under a rigid, padded counterpane, so far as I was able to tell fully-dressed, watching the spokes of light become harder-edged, deeper golden, better-defined; listening to the haloed, picking up, quickening sounds of London at six o'clock.

I was at The Quoag, better known as Bobby's, the (very) short-stay hotel popular for generations with people meeting for 'funch' – lunchtime fucking, with blank receipts from the fishing-net-and-raffia-nested-chianti-bottle restaurant on the ground floor – 'moodies' – provided *tout compris*, so that the knobbing was eventually reimbursable as a justifiable business expense.

There was a hot wire piercing my thalamus, hypothalamus, parietal cortex and limbic system, so that I didn't dare raise my head above the horizontal. But lying flat made me feel something life-threatening was about to take place in the ribs region: there were fluids sluicing around my upper body, swamping my heart (what I judged to be my heart), which itself felt inflated, spongily engorged, when I was lying down. Something that I remember thinking seemed like orange juice seemed to be trickling out of my nose.

The next time I woke, the lines of light were ticking across the ceiling with more purpose, indicating that the traffic had thinned. It was probably about 2 a.m. and I had wiped out almost a whole twenty-four hours. I risked sliding a few inches up the head-board and, with my left hand, groped inside the bedside cabinet. This happened, conveniently, to be a minibar, and I came up with some foil-wrapped peanut brittle and some International Party Mix in a five-ounce ring-pull can. When I had taken care of these (leaving aside the seaweed-glazed Japanese crackers, which I have never liked), it seemed to make some of the sense of panic paralysis recede.

An hour, perhaps two hours later, it occurred to me to slip the trousers I had been sleeping in under the mattress, in an effort to get them to look at least half-decent when it was time to leave. I succeeded in kicking them off and folding them and arranging them more or less flat without glimpsing any evidence of the lowering brown oceans and exotic archipelagos of human stains. In the course of this (in the circumstances) tricky manoeuvre, though, my eye was drawn into the dark crevice of the bucking tongue, the throat where mattress peeled away from base and where I spied the dim, dog-eared, delaminated surface of what could only be porn. I plucked it from its hiding place, catching a confirming drift as I did so of the lewd inks, and fell back in the bed with all the dry-mouthed excitement of a secret debauche.

Every page showed a pie-faced woman in congress with a German Shepherd or a Borzoi, frequently both. She wore a short brown wig in some pictures, engineer boots and a zippered leather mask in others; only from the dusting of acne on her pale adipose buttocks – acne like a map of the cosmos; galaxies and galaxy clusters, conurbations of stars – was it possible to confirm that it was the same person.

I fell into a fitful sleep in which I dreamed of babies, dolls, disease, the corruption of the body – the things that go bad in the world of time, and decay. I woke with my face an inch or so from the wall, where, written in a tiny Rapidographic hand just below the lower edge of the paper dado (laurel garlands, prancing elegant-necked gazelles), I read the following: 'Lipstick on a penis/a kiss on a running sore/ sadness, madness, melancholy, and despair'.

– 'Generally, by the time you are Real, most of your hair has been loved off, and your eyes drop out and you get loose in the joints and very shabby. But these things don't matter at all, because once you are Real you can't be ugly, except to people who don't understand.'
– 'I suppose you are Real?' said the Rabbit. And then he wished he had not said it, for he thought the Skin Horse might be sensitive. But the Skin Horse only smiled.
– 'The Boy's Uncle made me Real,' he said. 'That was a great many years ago; but once you are Real you can't become unreal again. It lasts for always.'

I remember my father describing to me once how the men of his regiment, himself included, had looted the homes of innocent Dutch families during the liberation of Holland. This was in '44 or '45, just before the end of the war, when the ordinary squaddie hadn't experienced home, and the comforts of home, for many months, in some cases years.

It wasn't valuables they looted, but the simple *heimelig* objects that they associated with peace and stability and physical and spiritual ease: sideboards, armchairs, those fringed chenille table coverings with depictions of windmills and dumpling-cheeked little dyke-pluggers in turned-up-toed clogs that you still find in some older Dutch bars today; they even took hearth-rugs and cheap mantel ornaments. The brass went hairless when they found the dug-outs converted into room-sets of cosy front parlours in Sunderland and Birmingham and Stepney. But they did nothing, because they could see the men were in the mood to kill rather than surrender the right to enjoy these potent reminders of a normal human existence.

Everybody can always use a little Christmas, as Frank Sinatra once said, explaining why he keeps Christmas-tree lights burning in his house all the year round. Even Ronnie Duncan — big, don't-piss-on-my-back-and-tell-me-it's-raining, rooted-in-the-world Ronnie Duncan, forcibly uprooted from the mess of his desk and the fortress of his office and the consolations of nicotine, now the building is a smoke-free, open-plan, virtually paper-free zone — Ronnie Duncan has lately taken to towing a small module behind him as he moves about the office making his executive pronouncements. Officially, this cabinet-on-wheels is supposed to contain all the bumf the new clean-desking mandates prohibit him from leaving lying around the place. Unofficially, it is no accident that he now looks like a small child pulling a favourite choo-choo or tottering cube of alphabet blocks on a trolley, or that he appears indifferent to this childhood regression. (Many people have remarked on how unhyper, how eerily unlike himself he has been seeming lately.)

I couldn't have foretold that a fluffy toy given to me more than two years earlier by the wife of a serial child killer would be what I would reach for — something cuddly and sterile and acquainted with death — when life once again belly-upped and went weird on me. But this is what I asked Myc Doohan to go to my flat and get, when I eventually tracked him down. (He had spent the morning covering the opening by the Duke of Edinburgh of one of the new upgraded Poly-Universities — somebody back at the ranch's idea of a joke.) Mrs N would give him the keys; he'd find the little dog in question by a stack of mouldering newsprint between the Exercycle (broken) and the window, abandoned but unresentful, an expression of absolute, insatiable neediness on its come-all, forgive-all machine-made face.

Doohan was the one person I could trust to do this who wouldn't make unhelpful suggestions. (Like: Are you sure you wouldn't rather have me call a doctor? Or: Wouldn't you prefer to be oiled and stroked to orgasm by a topless lady of your choice?) A man who spends his mornings strapping himself into a whalebone corset (couturièred by the London woman who post-operatively resculpted Andy Warhol and President Reagan among others), and his nights wanly communing with the oily city river is a man chasing his own demons. I also knew that Doohan was somebody who wouldn't risk even a trip to the new University of the Outer Circle without taking his own charms and amulets with him:

a brass pixie, a four-leaf clover, two silver dollars, a dashboard Jesus, and two St Christophers in case one was more effective than the other. ('Oh world, world, world, wondrous and bewildering, when did my troubles begin?')

It was around one, I was vegging into day two of my occupancy of that twilit, garlic-reeking knocking shop, when I heard a key slip into the lock and opened my eyes to see an apprehensive – a frankly spooked – Doohan making his entrance. Hoisted on the heels of his tan cowboy boots, the kneed and bunched trousers of his suit dragging, thin hair slapped against his scalp, glasses steamed, the buckled belt of his leather coat trailing the floor, Doohan looked as if he had been bin-diving with the aristocracy of the gutter in Leicester Square. The paper sack in which he carried his belongings was sodden and collapsing; the newspapers clamped under his arm were flopping grey pulp; the little dog looked like a consolation prize from budget bingo in its patchily opaque, dingy shroud. 'I'll just do a piss,' Doohan said, disappearing into the bathroom, and re-emerged gulping on a joint.

He paced the floor at the foot of the bed, lugubriously filling me in on the trade gossip I'd missed over the previous twenty-four hours: who was up, who was down, who was stuffing who. He had had a telephone conversation earlier that morning with a young photographer he had never met who he was meant to be working with for the first time. 'I'm five-foot-eight, clean-shaven, ponytail, that kind of genre,' the smudger had told him. 'I'll be with an assistant, blonde, of the female persuasion. You'll be carrying a pineapple, I presume.' ' "My assistant," ' Doohan said. 'What happened to aiming it, holding the bleedin' thing steady and pressing the tit? Probably still crapping his nappies this time last year. The wank in the bath.'

And meanwhile the reason for Doohan's mercy dash loomed between us, heavy-handed, unalluded to, mute. Doohan had deposited the dog on the bed without saying anything. I watched him concentrate on not looking at it the way you consciously try to stop your eye straying to somebody's facial tic or intriguing stain or unusual physical deformity. A single smut had penetrated the factory wrap and lodged itself on the velvety muzzle. Otherwise it had made it this far unscarred and unblemished; it was a clean slate, an empty vessel.

I looked at Doohan: winded; shot; his future behind him. I thought of the pair of us: the bad-news bears, the bathos junkies. We had started out so well. But something in our lives had brought us to this pass: two middle-aged men in a cheapjack hotel doing a ten-minute fandango around the cuddly creature one of them has become convinced possesses the magic necessary to deliver some tragically mislaid part of himself back to himself. I wasn't ready to take up my bed and walk out of the room and at the same time was convinced I couldn't spend another hour there without this primitive contrivance.

Doohan offered me a hit on his joint. I declined. He inhaled it down to the filter, flushed the roach down the toilet, then shambled about gathering together his sodden bits and pieces. 'I've seen rough, but you look dog rough,' he offered as a parting shot. 'Thanks, Myc,' I said. 'I'll do the same for you one day.' He made the peace sign when all that remained visible of him was one hand extended through a gap in the door.

The condolence card with the swallows and Rachel Stires's lines of doggerel on it had unstuck itself somewhere along the line and gone missing. The glue of the crimp-seal around the dog gave way easily with a soft hiss, a small aromatic explosion of polypropylenes and carbides, moth-proofers, flame-retardants, bonding agents, synthetic fur and filling. The facial features were folkloric, uniform, idealised, designed to punch all the age-old buttons. They didn't ask anything specific, or say anything specific; they encouraged the owner – and I acknowledged that that was me now – to bring them to life by projecting the specific onto them. They were full of empty content, waiting to be filled.

The chemical aromas diffused quickly. This was never a toy that was going to be invested with the warm milky smell of a child. It had evaded the wet earth and keening laments of its intended destination. Now as my life's companion it was going to be filled with my smell: the smell of sour nightsweats, flopsweat, piney Karvol, gaseous emissions, and the mulchy, bubbling-under sub-odours of disgust, disappointment, fatigue and panic.

I was timid at first about any overt display of affection. What a snooper lens couldn't do with a snoutful of this. A frame-by-frame account of my slow-motion private smash-up. A gift for somebody with an eye for the grotesque and gamey. A Weegee, a Louis Liotta, an Arbus, a Heath Hawkins. (Caption: 'His/Her central concern remained unwavering – it focused on the nature of being alone and our pitiful range of attempted defences against it.') I glanced at the window. The blind remained lowered. Tentatively at first, I let my nose graze in the semi-lush, machine-cropped fabric. I was covered all over in a thin film of perspiration. I made myself familiar with the bunched legs, investigated the raggedy outsize ears. Then I tucked the little dog under my chin and drifted into the sweetest sleep with my arms clamped close around it.

When I woke up I was irrationally (childishly) upset not to find it where I had left it. It took a minute or two to locate it under the bedclothes, snug in the hollow made by my drawn-up, foetal knees. It took me back to the days when a Townsend terrier called Ali used to burrow his way into the bed in the mornings and make a space for himself between me and Even. And further back to when I was a child, when my mother would wrap a hot water bottle up in an old cardigan before slipping it into the arctic sheets, a cooling core of heat encrypted in the leaden blankets.

It was only when I retrieved it that I noticed the maker's label sewn into a body-seam: *Fullalove*. And on the reverse: 'Eternitoys (Div. of Jaykay Group), Vallance House, Vallance By-Way, Sleaford. Upkeep: minimal. Shelf-life: eternal.'

F : O : U : R

Day 24. I ask Heath Hawkins a question, one I have long wanted to ask him.

We are in what Hawkins usually refers to as his 'hooch' (a hangover from the Vietnam days) – actually the bottom half of a battered/bijou property in an SW postal district popular with dumbed-down, cokehead trustafarians, and older BMW-bohemians like himself. (I make it that Heath must be fifty-seven now.)

The air is incense-rich, the lighting strained through flimsy pieces of ikat and paisley and tie-dye fabric that have been weighted with glass beads and cowries and draped over the shades of the lamps. There is a low table with the figure of Ganesh, the elephant Buddha, on it, along with a row of lard-like ecclesiastical candles. The candles illuminate a Tibetan mandala whose circular pattern turns out, when you get close to it, to consist of ingeniously interlocked copulating figures. One third of the room has an icy, Insectocutor-blue caste as a result of the light falling into it from the adjacent room whose walls are lined with tanks containing puffers, tangs, blue-face angels, moray eels and other slyly darting tropical fish.

None of this, though, is what visitors to Heath Hawkins's house tend primarily to remember. In an act of contamination or transference, the images they take away with them when they leave are the sepulchral, transfixing, bottom-of-life images that Heath's shutter has opened up over the years to let in. This gallery of the dead and dying, the bestial and the grotesque – a few of the pictures framed, most enlarged and then simply taped or pinned to the walls; all of them in black-and-white – doesn't appear to have been assembled so much as to have self-spawned organically, like a bacterial invasion, or a flocky pattern of cumulus damp.

Before me where I am standing is an image from his notorious (unpublished) post-mortem portfolio. The corpse is that of a middle-aged woman whose head is turned to one side and buried in shadow. The incision that has been made from the throat to the pubic bone is in the process of being stitched up, with coarse dragging stitches. Clearly visible in the open stomach cavity is the cigarette Hawkins had been smoking a couple of seconds before he took the picture. Seeing him looking around for an ashtray, he has told me, the mortuary assistant, the only other person present, had taken the cigarette from him and casually stuffed it into the woman's belly.

Above this picture is the picture of a spliff-toting GI, his face painted up for night walking, around his neck a necklace of eleven human tongues. Below it, the picture of Walter Brand that Heath snatched in The Cherry and Fair Star three or four nights ago, and next to this an equally unforgiving studio portrait, a posed picture of Walter, his old *cajones* hanging low in, his arthritically ballooned knees exploding out of, a pair of his late wife's precious silk knickers.

Proceeding in a clockwise direction around the room we find blowups of:

– an amputee in Yemen having the pulp of his shoulder wound cauterised with red-hot irons

– a girl holding a doll giving birth to another doll

– a naked Heath Hawkins photographed by himself, the fat-lipped black lesions articulating the surface of his body like leeches

– a group of children hideously impaled on a column of concertina razor wire in a public square in Saigon; the razor wire encircles their father, a formally dressed man, who is facing execution

– a young black revolutionary being necklaced with a blazing rubber tyre in one of the townships in South Africa

– Linzie's, Hawkins's first wife's, sutured and fisted mastectomy scar

– one of the ninety-five Liverpool football fans who died at Hillsborough, the grid-pattern of the boundary fence against which the life was crushed out of him branded on his face. (Hawkins had had to flip the body with his foot where it was lying on the pitch, something he had done many times in combat situations. Here, though, it had almost sparked a mini-riot, a small turbulence inside the greater turbulence)

– two men, the uncle and grandfather, gazing at the four fingers of a small girl which have just been chopped off by her mother

– a black vulture with human fat coursing down its feathers and tatters of knobby flesh hanging loose from its mouth, snapped in a border village during the Indo-Pakistan War

Life with the crusts on, as Heath has a fondness for saying. Life with the crispyfuckincrusts on, man.

'Tell me,' I say to him. 'I've always wanted to know. Do you ever get, you know . . . the horn on, taking pictures of this stuff?'

I'm drinking Belikin ('Belize's #1 beer' according to the label) out of the bottle. Hawkins is crouched over a table, engrossed in his crack paraphernalia. 'Yeah, man,' he says. 'You shitting me?' He has a jerried-together 'works' consisting of a plastic Pepsi bottle, some perforated tin foil and an empty biro casing. He makes some final, fiddling adjustments: grouting, tapping, tamping. Then there is a big druggy moment – a hallowed hiatus – while he takes the smoke deep down into his lungs. A sooty deposit blooms inside the bottle; his face is obscured momentarily by a duster of dirty grey smoke. There is a loud exhale. 'Mmmmm,' he says, before this thickens into a cough. 'Oh yeah! Major chubbies. But *major* chubbies.'

Heath is wearing a pair of tiger-stripe fatigues with soft-soled Gucci moccasins and a white T-shirt with a small NASA emblem on it. He'll put on a caramel-coloured cashmere jacket before we leave.

'Don't be such a chickenshit, Normsky, try some,' he says, already preparing more 'rock' in the microwave. I hold up the beer bottle, indicating that I'm happy with what I've got. 'Okay, once a juicer, always a juicer. I know. But here's a medicament which allows you to seize control of your pilot light. I'm depending on you not to punk out on me tonight. You're not going to punk out on me, are you? Here. Have a hit. Just to be sure. Put the glide back in your stride. Feel what it's like to burn with a hard gem-like flame for once, instead of guttering like an old smudgepot. Guaranteed orbit. Blow your head off.'

Heath is in business in this area in a modest way, scoring cocaine, crack, ecstasy, ganja for friends, and (surprisingly thoroughly) checked-out friends of friends. The revenue is useful, but he says (and I believe him) that it is the 'conspiratorial ambience' he is hooked on and that he looks to to keep an edge. There have already been a couple of inept coded telephone conversations in the brief time I've been here about 'aunty' coming for 'tea' and the time that tea will be poured. Hawkins happily admits that he is paranoid, and sleeps with a loaded M-2 carbine and a machete under his bed.

The patterns on the well-worn rugs scattered around and on the loose covers on the furniture suggest the inscribed façades of mosques and Mayan temples; Berber tattoos. 'X' (I mention the name of another blood-and-guts photographer we both know) 'puts his pictures away under lock and key every night so their souls can't get at him.'

Surprisingly, this fails to raise the expected derisory rasp. 'They are the denizens of the other world. They seem to be looking back at us from some other place, as though to tell us something. The dark seamy corners, the neglected populations. You have to get close enough to get the picture, but get too close and you die.'

Heath has started strapping his hands with green gaffer tape, having first prepared twelve-inch strips of tape which he has stuck all along the edge of the table, like a seasoned corner man. Before embarking on this, he distributed lens caps, rolls of film, light metres and other pieces of necessary equipment around the cargo pockets of his fatigue pants. This has given him an awkward, padded-out look, but inside it he still looks limber, kick-box thin. He shrugs into his jacket; takes a last deep inhale of the joint he has had going to even out the buzz of the crack cocaine. 'Right,' he says. 'Time to move this gig east.'

We are halfway to the door when he remembers he has forgotten something. He retrieves the small velvet draw-string bag which has been hanging around the neck of the elephant Buddha, and loops it over his own head, a gesture he has perfected so that there is not a chance of him disturb-ing his hair. 'Benign senescent forgetfulness. Long-term brain fade,' he groans. 'Jeezus Godhelpus. Okay. Dead-body detail time, this time. Let's make some frames.'

We are in the golden valley – the valley of goods and services, lights and signs, two undifferentiated, pin-hole lights our-selves in the sequined belt of lights as monitored by the Met's traffic blimp or helicopter hovering overhead. The only easy route to where we are going is through the business ghetto, with its simple planar geometry, its hard-landscaping and bold international symbols; its developing security presence – uniformed men at desks keep coming up like pictures in a flicker book as the lights go on and a hazy summer dusk deepens. I see us reflected side by side in the curtain walls, woozily distorted by the mirage ripples and subtle dents, Heath Hawkins driving. The surge, and the dawdle, a country song (another country song) – 'By day I make the cars, by night I make the bars' is how this one goes – on the tape.

As proof that we are moving, department-store windows begin to offer blazing clement weathers, the inevitable colourful abundance: nipples pushing against sheer fabric as if exposed to a cross-draught, skirts pinned and petrified to look as if they are being lifted on the wind; the almost familiar faces, the nearly convincing wigs. And in the doorways, the collateral damage of advanced urban life, preparing a bed for the night: the hingeless and the homeless, with their harmonicas and bongos and layered filth, their community spirit and scurf-necked patient dogs.

Buoyed on the sounds of Memphis and Nashville, we glide by rape sites and murder sites, scenes of hit-and-runs, child snatches, vendetta assassinations, carjackings, care-in-the-community neck stabbings, and their commemorative shrines in varying conditions of completion – the full gamut, from newly layed and composting flowers, to cinderblock bunkers with decorative ironwork grilles and creosoted roofs, plastic bouquets in Third World vases, flickering candles, Christmas lights, bottles and mirrors to deflect the remaining malignant spirits, and pictures of the deceased hologramically – *hyperdelically* – rendered or cheaply photocopied and sheathed in plastic.

And then the angle of elevation changes and we soar into an aerial shot – up onto the ribboned flyover, forced all at once up close against cluttered bedsits (collapsed suitcases, string-tied boxes forced into the spaces between ceilings and wardrobes; thin partitions bisecting windows, interposed between sinks and beds, quarantining weary soul from weary soul); then the italic signs and steamy sculleries and rookeries, the staff kennels of chain hotels; the stepped terraces, industrial clerestories and diagonal zoots of the eighties economic miracle; the decorative Arab fascia and stylised Native American motifs. 'London,' Heath exults, nose pointed roofwards, both hands off the wheel. 'The planet's heart chakra.'

The press pen opposite St Saviour's is only sparsely populated – it's pub time; several pairs of aluminium ladders lean against the barriers, labelled as to newspaper, padlocked and chained. Opposite, under the vertebra'd white canopy of the hospital, Scott McGovern's fan base is holding up. After three weeks, you could reasonably expect some evidence of erosion or attrition, some bowing to the demands of hearth and home. Instead, the women resonate with a sense of power and purpose, daily reinforced by repetitive chant and prayer, rhythmic ceremony and song – the raisers of megaliths, the builders of henges.

At the rear of the hospital, a pair of tall metal gates swing open, permitting us entry to a loading and delivery area. The gates grind shut behind us, and a light on a security camera mounted above a row of industrial dumpsters blinks from amber to red. The bulky silhouette of a man appears briefly in a lighted doorway at the end of the yard, and then the door clicks closed again. There are diamond-shaped reflector signs saying 'Hazchem' and 'Bio-hazard'. Vehicular weight has ploughed ruts into the bricks of recently laid York stone. Bluish puddles have collected in the depressions. We wait in silence.

'Time-lapse recorders maintain up to 749 hours of images on a two-hour cassette,' Heath eventually says. He has begun chopping lines of coke on a flat mirror compact he has fished out of a coat pocket, using the edge of a credit card. 'It's obvious – isn't it? – that the purpose of surveillance devices is to *create* suspicious behaviour, rather than detect it. We are witnessing the development of an environment almost wholly owned and managed by a corporate hegemony. Machine eyes are objects gathering information.' There are four lines, two apiece. When we have finished, he collects stray particles from the mirror and the edge of the Optima card with his middle finger and rubs them along the line of his gums. He runs a check on his nostrils in the rear-view mirror, then unrolls and pockets the twenty note I have given him, the second time this has happened tonight, but I say nothing.

We listen to the traffic noise; the lilting music of a distant hymn being sung by the women. There is a deep-down, basso profundo thunderous sound, and we vector away from each other and – after all these years – crane our heads sideways to catch a glimpse of Concorde going over. It is a commonly observed part of the London day: people stopping in parks and on streets and bridges to stare at the sky and watch Concorde's trajectory of takeoff or descent, some transported by the clean lines, the sense of technological can-do; most alert for signs of wobble or falter, practising how to describe the way it just turned into a plummeting ball of flame. 'How d'you always know a guy coming towards you is wearing his hair in a ponytail?' Heath says in the reverberating silence. 'You can't *see* anything. But you always know, right?'

He checks the time on his watch against the time on the dashboard clock and puts something that looks like a prayer shawl around his neck to conceal his cameras. The video camera begins a silent oscillation and, at the signal from the fat man, who has reappeared, we make a crouched run for it down the yard, keeping our heads below the beam of the motion detector, like visiting firemen in one of the world's trouble-spots, weaving to avoid sniper fire from rebel groups in the mountains. 'This is Charlie,' Heath says when we are in and the fat man has secured the door behind us. 'Charlie will give you some good shit. Charlie will fill up your notebook big-time.'

Because it is a new hospital (new, that is, in terms of the

fabric: a hospital has stood on this site since the early nine-teenth century), the security at St Saviour's is considered state of the art. The incidence of mad axe-men and maternity-ward prowlers and syringe-wielding orderlies, of bogus doctors performing high-risk peritonology, heroic neurosurgery, splashy angioplasties, has meant that security at all hospitals in the last few years has had to be stepped up.

And then of course there are the people like us – people like Heath and me. It used to be easy-peasy; a piece of pure piss: a pair of overalls and a pot of paint, or a Black and Decker and a Woodbine behind the ear and, bingo, you were in. A couple of stunts have been pulled since Scott McGovern was laid low: somebody posing as a junior doctor and demanding to see his notes; somebody else having flowers delivered to another patient on McGovern's floor, with the number of his newsdesk and some money con-cealed. But these were gestures that owed more to a nostalgia for the old ways than any real expectation of a result.

Now that we have crashed it, I have a vivid sense of us as migratory tumours or parasite invaders, unwelcome boarders being scanned by the hospital surveillance apparatus in the way advanced imaging techniques hunt down a pocket of pus or a locus of inflammation in the body's dark halls and caves. Hawkins thinks we will simply be carried from the point of ingress to our eventual destination like cellular debris riding the rapids of the lymph channel before passing poison-ously into the flowing stream. Put it down to the amounts of substances consumed.

Like Clit Carson, the part of the hospital where we pres-ently find ourselves doesn't officially exist. According to the plan which is available for public consumption, the area that makes up Charlie's night-time kingdom consists of a lecture theatre, administration offices, and storage. This leaves about a half of the square-footage unaccounted for, a blank on the chart, where you will in fact find the morgue and the post-mortem room, a sluice room, a furnace room, a number of side-rooms filled with the honest brightness of clamps, scalpels, kidney-shaped bowls, hydraulic corpse technology. This is the place where death is − the incipient organic decay, the mephitic odours; the place where the bodies come.

It is also where Heath comes, when word reaches him that they have got something good in. In the way certain waiters at certain restaurants, and certain doormen at certain hotels, get on the blower to the paparazzi when they've 'trapped', so Hawkins has established a small network of morgue minders and corpse handlers who bell him when they have anything noteworthy in the way of physical peculiarities or deformities, interesting examples of scarification, mutilation, post-mortem carnivore chewing, branding, tattoos. Tattooing − stigmataphilia − is Heath's current area of special interest, combining, as he believes it does, secret ritual, traditional art, physical pain and sensual pleasure. St Saviour's in recent months has produced a man with a life-size portrait of himself apotheosised as an angel in multi-coloured inks on his back, and another man whose back was completely covered with a tattoo version of the poster of a ball-fondling, bare-buttocked woman in a tennis dress, popular among chem-eng students in the nineteen-seventies.

This sequestered place is actually on the ground level of the building, although the absence of windows gives it an airless, basement feel. Visitors go up a curved ramp to the main first-floor entrance at the front of the hospital − currently home to the McGovern faithful. The walls are battleship grey, the ceilings low and pipe-lined, dull bulkheads.

139

There are stainless steel anti-scuff panels at waist-height that hardly show any sign of wear. The composition floor is embedded with a kind of silver-gold microglitter whose dancing liveliness seems inappropriate in such a place, like giggling in church.

We file in and follow Charlie down a shallow, rubber-covered incline. A bad smell drifts back from Charlie – formalin? ether? whisky? the smell that comes from prolonged exposure to evisceration and dismemberment? Flesh lies in folds at the back of his neck, and judders at every jarring footfall. Flesh billows around the armpits of the hospital-issue uniform, sagging and moving like breasts.

We keep following Charlie past a room piled with used bandages and dressings, an alcove lined with *boudins* and cutlets in bottles, and have just passed a scullery area containing rigid white plastic aprons and calf-length rubber boots when Heath suddenly stops. 'Can you hear that?' He is standing under the metal panel of an air intake or ventilation duct. 'Here. Cop a listen. Pretty nutso, what d'you think? But you *must* hear,' he says, when I tell him all I'm hearing is the sound of liquid draining into metal pans. 'You don't hear them? The murmuring souls? The howls of the unburied? The souls condemned to wander unhappily until their mortal remains have been laid to rest? That weird wilderness sound? Well, there it is, Normsky, there it is.'

We turn left into a concrete hall, and catch up with Charlie who is standing by a central refrigerator containing sixty drawers. A red digital readout flickers as the temperature rises and falls: 35 degrees, 36, 35. The walls are tiled in swimming-pool blue, and dim grids of fluorescent light hang from the ceiling. I don't notice it at first, but one of the drawers is open on the second tier, and inside it is a woman's leg lying on white gauze, flaccid, marbled, slightly bent at the knee. It immediately reminds me of the party shop near where I live, and the row of inflated legs doing a jerky can-can in the window twenty-four hours a day, round the clock, non-stop. No doubt it reminds Hawkins of something else: of Khe San and Qui Nhon and Hue, body parts in the branches of trees, dead Vietnamese with lighted cigarettes and worse pushed into the slots of their mouths.

There is a blackening red stain on the gauze where bone and marbled muscle tissue protrude from the thigh. Charlie says the leg was found in a London canal and will be given its own funeral – buried so that it can be exhumed if necessary, in a coffin, with a priest present. Hawkins, who doesn't judge it to be worth even a frame, propels the drawer shut with his knee. 'I think,' he says to Charlie, 'that we're looking for something off your top shelf.'

Charlie goes to fetch a trolley, and Hawkins drifts over to some lift doors wide enough to accommodate entire life-support systems; beds complete with IV tubes, heart monitors, traction counterweights, none of which, being surplus to requirements, ever get as far as this floor. He seems convinced that the shaft is also a conduit for whatever it was he thought he was hearing a few minutes ago. 'Don't tell me you don't hear this,' he says. 'It sounds like some deep-space receiver picking up fragments of communication flows from Earth. Sobbing whispers heard deep in the jungle at night, howls carried on the wind, trees and plants moaning in awful harmony. Tribal people calling to each other through the manioc leaves in the jungle of screaming souls.'

Charlie has wheeled the cadaver into the post-mortem room, where you get a better light. Slipping his hands under the back and knees, he log-rolls it onto a ribbed dissecting table made of stainless-steel, not caring whether he minimises the degree of bounce or not. He peels back the sheet to reveal a face in sublime repose; in a state of almost seraphic innocence which belies its owner's reputation as one of the major hate figures of the day. We all know the background, but Charlie proceeds to run us through it anyway, determined to give value, like a tour guide at a cash-strapped stately home, or somebody on television describing the chesterfield sofa that is the day's star prize.

What we have in front of us is a bozo who got his kicks from preying on elderly people living alone. He was wanted on charges of burglary, vicious assault, sodomy and rape when his stepmother, certain he was the man that police were seeking, went into his bedroom while he was sleeping and stabbed him once, expertly through the heart.

Hawkins has wandered off halfway through Charlie's recital, and has been standing with an ear pressed against the gap in the lift doors. 'It was a small town in the forest with a lake and a fishing fleet and many ox wagons and rickshaws and bicycles. Most of the houses had walls made from long, braided leaves of a reed that grew by the river, and roofs woven from palm fronds,' he begins once Charlie has finished. 'Through lanes among the houses ran children and stubby-legged short-haired dogs. Profuse schools of fish arrived in the river during high water. As the river withdrew, they were confined to ponds in the fields; the villagers caught them in buckets. The days were always hot, and in the air was the damp fertile smell of the river.'

He picks up a wooden block with a half-circle cut out of it and brings it to where we are standing in the light, either side of the dissection table. 'Our world is networked together using small mouth noises, which are speech, or symbols for small mouth noises,' Heath says. 'This is not a wide band for communication, this small mouth-noise thing.'

He slips the block under the dead man's heavy head, and crouches low over him with his Leica, bionic taped hands and taped camera working together like a single piece of integrated machinery. Rimed in coke sweat, elbows planted either side of the body, Heath goes in tight on the words that are banner-printed across the forehead, tattooed an inch above the eyes: 'Made in England 1965'.

A blob of perspiration rolls off his chin and quickly spreads to a button-size stain on the shroud. He stands, works his shoulders until they crack loudly, mops his face with the corner of the teatowel-like keffiyeh. 'And so,' he says with an exaggerated autocutie leer. 'We come to the main award of the evening.'

The door to the service stairs, activated by Charlie with his card-key, had opened with a depressurised suck or pop which started a tonal pulse that rapidly increased in volume and didn't stop until the door had been secured behind us. Except it didn't exactly seem to stop so much as fade into a loop of related, repetitive electronic sounds. These have been combined with tribal music – reed flutes, chimes and gourds – and overlaid with the sound of rainwater dripping and trickling off ferns, birds chirping, insects buzzing, what could easily have been the amplified heartbeats of tiny animals; plaintive yodels and chants. 'The sound of sad, open spaces. Weird echoes. The mantle of the warm jungle,' Heath says. 'They shot the water buffaloes, the pigs and the chickens. They threw the dead animals into the wells to poison the water. Dinks, slopes, slants, gooks.'

Charlie and I have reached the level of the main reception area. Heath is squatting on a stone landing one flight down, doing another couple of lines. One of the original oratories at St Saviour's has been retained in the new design, the domed lead roof replaced with glass, and a rain forest environment of fan palms, pincer vines and monkey grass created in interlocking raised beds in the space underneath it. The yellow double-arch of a McDonald's dominates the figure-eight-shaped concourse that has resulted: there is the neon doodle of a 'Knickerbox', the sign of the black horse illuminated over an automatic-teller machine, and all the usual high-street franchises and concessions – sited here not so much for reasons of customer convenience, I imagine, than as a loss-leading therapeutic strategy, a business-caring-for-you distraction from the nearness and inevitability of personal death.

We are witness to all this through the kind of candy-stripe, one-way mirror that induces reflexive guilty behaviour (Heath's point) in customs halls and baggage reclaim areas. Two Indian women are steering wide-headed squeegee mops past the streamers of toilet paper that have been laid over a broken trail of vomit, their fuchsia and lime-green saris flowering exotically from the knee-length stems of nylon overalls. A yellow-faced man with a woollen cellular blanket safety-pinned at his chest waves goodbye to a visitor and begins wheeling himself back to his ward. A man comes in carrying a boxed pizza on the flat of his hand and paces in front of the lifts. A boy surreptitiously gouges a hole with a penknife in a moulded plastic seat.

There are plastic surfaces dressed in the appearances of other materials: quarried stone and endangered hardwoods; Dolomitic rock. The 'architected' rain forest muzak leaks from here to every part of the building via shafts and trunking and ducts. There is a perspex cube mounted on a pedestal nearby containing ropes of Mardi Gras beads, a comb, golf tees, toy wheels, a piece of rope, balloons, a plastic toothpaste cap, baggies, a plastic flower – the contents, Charlie says, of the stomach of a twelve-pound sea turtle that crawled onto a beach in Honolulu and died.

Now even as we are watching, the lighting dims, rises a few points, then stabilises at around the balming level expected in restaurants and wine-bars at this time of night. Scott McGovern's face is reversed and back-lit on the posters taped against the windows; the low sandbagged figures of the women keeping their vigil on the ramp swim into focus. It is as if they have stepped out of their lives; surrendered themselves to an event for which none of the rules and experiences of their previous existence has prepared them. They are dead to the mundane, to real-world commitments and affiliations, and seem poised for an experience of trans-cendence or revelation.

On each floor, Charlie has to punch numbers in a lock to keep us rising through the building. Our footsteps echo on the stone. Perspiration courses through Charlie's hair, basting the ridges of fat around his neck. He has to stop every flight and a half or so to draw coolness from the walls into his back and palms and recover his breath. 'The palace of pain'. 'Pain Central'. These are Hawkins's nicknames for St Saviour's. And waiting while Charlie engages in his small struggle it is easy to imagine pain as part of the hidden infrastructure, conduited through the central service core with the water risers and electric cabling and information systems. Pain as information; pain pathways; localised centres of pain; the prolonged and inexpressible pain of cancer and burns and stroke, of the agonised bodies arranged in rows, waiting for the end of pain; for their white moment. The building pulsing with pain like a caved molar.

The floor numbers are painted by hand on the walls, bog-standard red on grey. When we reach 4, Charlie enters the four-digit code, then the two-letter codicil, and instructs us to wait until we get the signal from him to follow him through a second door which he opens with his computer card. 'Affirmative!' Heath giggles, sliding down the wall until he is resting on his haunches in this small air-pocket full of refrigerator hum and the smell of drying urine and disinfectant.

The fourth floor is the top floor of St Saviour's. This part of it is decorated in pale pink, mocha, and tangerine, like a fashionable hairdressing salon. The same colours are prominent in the geometrical pattern of the curtains hanging at the window panels of the individual, one- and two-bed intensive-care cubicles. A nine-inch, black-and-white Ikegami monitor is tucked into a corner of the nurses' station. It is when the picture on this flickers and switches to a set of doors reinforced with metal panels at the end of the corridor that Charlie, holding up two fingers to indicate that we have two minutes to do the necessary, gives us the all-clear.

Minimally prowed, subliminally contoured, the nurses' station wouldn't look out of place at a Club Class check-in or advertising agency reception area. It is unattended, but a waxed milk-shake carton is a sign of recent occupancy; a several-sizes-larger-than-lifesize Easter chick sits on top of a concertinaed wad of computer print-out. A single door is set into the recess directly behind the counter, and this is the door to Scott McGovern's room.

He is invisible at first, obscured by the armoury of hissing

and pistoned biotechnology ranged around the bed, submerged in the macaronic web of tubes dripping pain-killers,
system suppressors, blood thinners, and diuretics into his
body from above. Orange scribbles on a TV monitor show
that blood is still being pumped to the brain from the heart.
Green blips on another screen show the cerebral cortex
giving up the fight for control of the emotive, animal centres
in the deepest layers of the brain.

The bed is raised on blocks. Above and to either side of
the bed rises a reef of adorability and bright plush – fluffy
bunnies and cuddly puppies, orange jumbos, day-glo hippos,
slogan teddies, purple chimps; goblins and gonks in jaunty
kerchiefs, home-made vests and coats. Tier upon tier of
machine washability, lovability, coal-black noses, dark plastic
eyes.

An Alice-band incision runs from ear to ear across McGovern's shaved, naked head. His face seems at once palid and
inflamed, his lips and nailbeds blue. He has none of the
repose of the gerontomonster we have been peeping down-
stairs. He appears fugitive, agitated; mouth twisted, eyes
fixed in a dilated state of horror. The large fixed circles are
unresponsive even when the flash strobes violently against
the transparent plastic structure that sits over his face. It is
circular, like the spare-wheel cover on a Shogun or Subaru,
and one frame has convinced Hawkins that it has to go. He
rips it back where it is Velcroed around the perimeter, takes
a step back, and passes the umbilical flash attachment across
the bed to me.

'Higher. Hold it higher,' he orders after he has loosed off
a trial frame. 'Down a bit. Lower the angle. Straight at the
face. Great. One more. One more.' He is arched backwards,
leaning in with his body, leaning back with his head, giving

himself options, making optimum use of what can only be the sixty seconds remaining. I look at McGovern's head, light as a larva casing, hardly denting the pillow, inundated with light, derealised in brilliance. I look away. Hawkins's trousers are tented at the front, taut across his erection. 'We're nearly there. Right *at* the face,' he urges. 'We're there.'

My hands are perspiring. My sweaty prints are on the gun. My dabs. I'm in it up to the hilt. ('Let him have it, Chris.')

McGovern's face once shone with publicity – with the glamour and consciousness of advertising, of television, of innumerable photographs. And it still has an aura; it is still 'auratic', but in a different way: it has been unmade; unpackaged; it shines with the aura of death. With the disc of plastic back in place, it looks like a picture of itself; the picture we have just half-inched. It looks like the xeroxed photographs of the deceased that it has become the custom to slip behind the light-reflecting wrapping around carnations or roses left at the shrines.

'Good going. Nice job, boss. Wowsa, wowsa, wowsa,' Heath Hawkins says. Then: '*Hic est locus ubi mors gaudet succurso vitae*. Better believe it. This is the place where death rejoices to come to the aid of life.'

F : I : V : E

'Hurray!' thought the little Rabbit. 'Tomorrow we shall go to the seaside!' For the Boy had often talked of the seaside, and he wanted very much to see the big waves coming in, and the tiny crabs, and the sand castles.

When I was in the ascendant and the bean-counters in travel-and-accounting would call me Norman and visibly perk up a little when they encountered me in the lavatories and the corridors – jousting, joshing ('You did put an "X" for "no publicity" on that last expenses claim?') – in those days, I used to stay in the class of hotel, more-stars-than-the-Planetarium places, where the mirrors made you taller, thinner, bolder-outlined, more substantial; a real occupying presence. It is what you are paying over the odds for, this stroking. Mirrors that are flattering, magical and abracadabrant. Lighting that is sequenced, angled, theatrically filtered; lighting that makes the skin look simultaneously taut and pampered, inwardly glowing, washed with that heavily wedged, wintering-in-Cap d'Antibes money tone.

Now they – and 'they' are by and large the same people; the same spreadsheet tinkerers and calculator Liberaces; the same shiny-arsed sandwich-at-the-deskers – plough through guides and gazetteers making sure they put me into places where the mirrors are positioned to show you in the cruellest light; to creep up on you and catch you at the most lowering angles, zooming in on the rouches and swags of fat, the albinoid goose-fleshy skin, the smashed capillaries, all the things you have learned to assiduously avoid in the normal run of existence.

Places with alopecia candlewick on the beds and rooster-sized stains worked into the linty carpets. Places with no Chicken Noodle News to buoy you through the sleepless small hours; no cable porno, no dedicated showers, no minibar, no billing-back. Just the mournful kettle and the inviolable envelopes of Ovaltine and Nescafé; the fire-doors occasionally flapping; the old birdcage lift beginning its lurches through the building with the arrival of the kitchen staff around six.

Welcome, in other words, to the Duke Hotel, in Seaton, a once-popular (although never fashionable), now run-down seaside resort a little over two hours by changing-train from London.

I was only able to turn this into an overnight after a lot of wrangling; but my protestations about needing time to get behind the conventional faded exterior and soak up the atmospherics finally won the day. After a lightning assessment of the degree of dilapidation, then digging my furry friend out of the bag and propping him against my pillow, my search for atmosphere took me somewhere called Muffins Licensed Tea Rooms, where I ordered a high-tea of fried eggs, mushrooms on toast and a dab of baked beans, helped on its way with a couple of stiffening Stolly-tonics.

The Jack and Jill for this (a highly reasonable £8.73) I quarter-folded and added to the wadded ball of counterfoils and flimsies and bits of till roll for generally much smaller amounts that I have to collect for reimbursement purposes. A small humiliation that the graduate intake of slumming scribblers, the young tab hands, have made into a game. It has become a point of honour among them to only eat hamburgers, doner kebabs, pizza; to use the tube and the bus ('to one travel pass, £6.80', representing one week's travel) rather than taxis. A way of saying they are different from us. Bicycles. A tactic to assert their non-culpability. These are the ones who voted the newsroom, all editorial departments, the canteen smoke-free zones. Get up in the morning and run. Meet their deadlines. Spend lunchtimes on the treadmills and pec decks in Body Awake, the in-house multi-gym. Queue up to be congratulated on the effectiveness of their hygiene practice by the dentist who anchors his mobile surgery in the car park every Friday. Wander the building accessorised with half-litre bottles of Highland Spring and Evian, offering each other strips of sugar-free gum.

Seaton, as you can imagine, is full of narrow cafés and greasy-spoons, all advertising their pastie/sausage/chips/Devonshire cream tea combinations in consternated jailbird freehand across the surfaces of paper plates. (Those old notices I remember as a child: 'Customers are requested not to consume their own food on the premises.') I settled on Muffins partly for its linen service and olde wheel-back chairs and the 'Licensed' in the title, but also for its open aspect, the people-watching possibilities it offered, being situated at the top of the main shopping street of the town, overlooking a grassed-over roundabout with the stone figure of a local worthy on it, grandly gesturing, and, beyond that, the tilt of the sea.

For the last few miles of its journey into Seaton, the local train had followed the course of a wide brown estuarial river, the expanse of mudflats fanning wider as the river approached the sea. At every station it picked up or put down elderly people with elbow-clamp crutches and wheelie shoppers, the occasional boy or girl in school uniform. Then I began to notice the travellers, people in medieval, nearly caveman, garb, getting off and on. Scarificed faces; ears, eyebrows, noses pre-emptively barbed with tines, coils; untreated sheepskins lashed to their chests and lower legs; belts of hemp and string; beads and tribal pendants; buckled archers' thongs; woad in their rasta hair.

Rough encampments, little clusters of timber-and-corrugated-iron shacks, started to spring up between the railway and the river. Makeshift settlements of wheelless vans, converted railway carriages, tar-papered chicken huts and ex-army tents. Communal fires. Naked babies. Bandana-wearing scavenger dogs.

Muffins was double-fronted, the big corner windows expansively curved. And into these fisheye frames stepped pretty much the mix as I had witnessed it on the train: retirees, cave-dwellers, simpletons, schoolchildren on the wag. Now joined by: the single homeless, the lone-parent families (the paper's style book insists that we call them this, and it's catching), the unfit mothers, the problem mongrel broods who gravitate here in the winter, unfurl their sleeping bags in the hotels and holiday lets and b-and-bs, and work at keeping the killer cold from establishing a beach-head in their bones. Of course it is no longer winter. It is June, nearly July. Nearly high-season, in so far as you can conceive of anything rising higher than knee-level in such a blighted, light-flooded, end-of-the-line place. Time for them to move out and on. But move where? How?

They walk the streets carrying all they own in blankets, paper-wrapped bundles, black refuse sacks. Bundles balanced on bicycle saddles, wheeled in supermarket trolleys and lurching buggies. Battering husbands. Whippet wives. Babies in crooked glasses. Like some way-station in a border war; some refugee camp, the number for credit card donations flashed up on the bottom of the screen. Teenage grannies. Winterwear chopped, slashed, cannibalised for the summer. Skull-and-crossbones tattoos. Lost-to-the-world faces, in dream-sequence montage, swimming up to the menu card in Muffins' window, staring blankly, lips going, conjugating egg, sausage, beans, pot of tea/egg, sausage, chips, beans, pot of tea/egg, sausage, chips, beans, round of toast, pot of tea. Two, three faces looking together, grey dead eyes, mouths silently working.

After a while the door opened and a woman came into Muffins Licensed Tea Rooms. She had an old-fashioned chorus girl figure, one hand resting on the shoulder of a boy who must have been aged about eight or nine. 'You be a good boy,' she told him when he was seated by himself at a table. 'Jean will tell me if you haven't been good, won't you, Jean?' It was obviously a custody situation, with Muffins the transfer point between parents. He had blond hair cut high up the back of his head, and a sign around his neck which said: 'I only eat natural foods. Do not give me sweets or snacks.'

When Jean took my plate away, I saw that the placemat was a cork-backed photograph of the front of Muffins. There was the purple paintwork and the half-net curtains, and there in the left-hand window was the table where I was sitting. Except seated around it in the picture, stiffly animated for the local snapper, was a party of strangers — a sports-jacketed man and two smiling women.

For some reason, I found this deeply unnerving. I felt all the old demons stirring (mouth dry, heart hammering, numbness deadening the ends of my fingers when I paid the bill). Back at the hotel I took two Rohypnol and put the Rabbit on stand-by on the bedside table. Then I lay down with the little dog clutched close to me and grabbed some shut-eye.

It was dark when I woke, and close even with the window open. The sound of plates being scraped. The ping! of a bullet in a television western, a sound I hadn't heard for a long time. The smell of drains — sweet and foul; somewhere under or around that, the green flatulent smell of the sea.

The hotel bar was full of cockney noise; drum-tight beer bellies and hair lacquer, the men wearing the ties or jacket insignia of some club or fellowship or sporting association; the women in lobe-dragging chandelier ear-rings and carpet slippers.

I took in some pubs. The Broken Doll. The Barking Dog. The Tite Barnacles. People waiting for other people. People already securely in the brotherhood of the bar. People watching each other's drinks go down, hoping the other will drink faster. Hateful fuckers. Fault finders. Catalytic people persons. People wanting to connect, but not connecting, waiting for the alcohol to hit. People lean and young and unencumbered.

Gazing on other people's reality with curiosity, with detachment, with professionalism. 'What is coming into being, we apparently have here in this bay one of the best collection of birds in Britain, and we are now getting from all over the country wildlife, naturalism, God-knows-what.'

Somewhere I heard this. I made a mental note, later a physical one. The solitary walker reconnoitring, stalking. The voyeuristic stroller.

The Oceanarium. Closed. The band shell, paint scraping off in giant soft flakes. The swimming bath, closed because of a breach in the sea wall. The Cyclone, the big dipper that swoops on its stilts and disappears into the banks of ornamental shrubbery alongside the railway. 'Britain in Bloom' planted out in flowers. Birdsong echoing in the station. Nicely tanked. Zapp Zone, a games arcade. Fuel food in the Kashmiri Veranda, where they sit you in a waiting area with copies of *Watchtower*, *Hello!*, *Marie Claire*, and take your money before they seat you at a table. A nightcap in a lounge bar full of dolorous clanging industrial music, the disc-jockeys in their foxhole canopied by camouflage netting. I listened intently for something recognisable, a hook, a key. None was forthcoming. But people were on their feet, hearing through the chaos to some concealed meaning, thrash dancing.

'So, pal,' I said when I got in. 'What news from the Rialto?'

Vera Batchelor is her name, my reason for being in Seaton. Spelled – for reasons we haven't gone into yet; for reasons we might never know – Veorah Batcheller. Suggesting the slave states and dirt cabins of the deep South; a big-hipped Dixieland vigour and swagger; both seats in the bus. Which, needless to say, wasn't at all Mrs Batcheller's manner when she ventured to correct the version of her name as I had it in my notebook. This was hesitant, apologetic, distinctly English.

It happened a week ago, at the memorial to the murdered

policewoman, Yvonne Fletcher. Mrs Batcheller hadn't seemed perturbed by my silent sneaking up on her, or even my calling her by the name of my wife, who she doesn't resemble in any way. She had gone on collecting together the rubber bands, the slugs of moss she had prised from between the paving stones at the base of the memorial, the leaves she had removed from the lower stems of the roses she had brought, the dirtied Q-tips. She heaped all this in the centre of the paper the flowers had been wrapped in, and balled it up. She gave a securing half-twist to the caps and nozzles of the bleaches and detergents she had been using, then placed these in a bag with the words 'The Big Shopper' printed on it. The white stone seemed scoured and, in a way, reconsecrated; violation-proofed; purified. She made some ritual adjustments to the plants and flowers, then stood back for a few moments to appraise the order and symmetry she had accomplished.

The bag was heavy, but when I offered to take it for her she refused to let me, swapping it from one hand to the hand with a ruffled metallic hair-tidier around the wrist. It was hot, so she carried her jacket between the bag handles. The interior of the square was still full of lunching office workers and we crunched across the gravel, seeking out the blocks and tunnels of shade around the perimeter, two of the few people moving.

I remembered that a French writer once spent a whole novel recounting the day of a man who crosses the Luxembourg gardens in Paris on his way to see a doctor, runs into different people, watches them, and tries to reconstitute for each of them the experience we all have on the one hand of looking out onto the world, and on the other of being exposed to an internal reverie of images and fantasies. The simultaneity that makes us always somehow both inside and outside ourselves as we move about. I relayed all this to Veorah Batcheller not because I believed she would be interested so much as impressed by my bona fides and credentials. This was Carson with his buddhas and mystics and monks. People sat on benches with their eyes closed, faces angled to the sun. People lay on their backs on the grass, bagged remnants of their lunches lying beside them, glancing at their watches, deciding just five more minutes. I was saying that I was a cut above; that I was to be trusted, I wasn't out to do the usual monstering job. I had mumbled my name. I thought I saw a glimmer of recognition. I wondered about my breath.

'A faint evocation of a famous film actress in a small part in an early faded film.' This is a steal from Greene that I have resorted to on too many occasions in my hacking life to risk using it again in my weirding of Veorah Batcheller. It applied to a couple of the women occupying tables in the Fountain Room in Fortnums. But mostly they were Japanese, some Germans, French, Americans. The Fountain Room was VB's choice. That is, I teased out of her an admission that it was somewhere she had long wanted to go and had never been able to gather up the courage to go on her own.

She had read in a magazine that Adam Faith came there. That it was his home from home, business combined with pleasure, the place where everybody always knew where to get him. He was on first-name terms with the waitresses, who regarded him as their best tipper and favourite customer, almost a venerable West End institution.

It at least supplied us with a neutral topic of conversation, with enough by-ways, sidebars, and common reference that we were able to spin it out more or less for the duration. (Any mention of Yvonne Fletcher or pierced-penis rapists, any personal prying into the whys and whos and whats of her life, I knew at this point of course would be fatal. Don't scare the horses.)

She only wanted tea, and was thrown for a loop when the waitress offered her the choice of Darjeeling, Earl Grey, English Breakfast, camomile and half a dozen others. Her hand shot inside the black leather bag she was holding on her lap and stayed there, closed tight around a packet of cigarettes and a cigarette lighter (there was no smoking) until it was time to leave. I kept wishing that Adam Faith would walk in, or that I had some lubricious stories, some hair-raising insider gossip about him to pass on, but I didn't. I'd given her her first cause for disappointment.

She kept the left side of her face turned from me all the time we were together. But I didn't realise that was what had been happening until we said goodbye, outside in the slipstream of the surging pavement traffic on Piccadilly.

Veorah Batcheller is a woman I would say of about forty-six – shortish, plumpish (solid, pneumatic, though, not fat – *zoftick*), with something wistful and displaced in her conjunction with the world, like the women you see boarding buses in the early mornings, their tiredness pointed up rather than painted over, as they think, with lipstick and mascara. She has kind, anxious eyes, and 'well-planted', as the Swiss say, luxuriant hair that has been damaged by the processes that have given it its ferrous glints and fixed the long corkscrew curls that cascade, water-spaniel-like, around a face that is only just beginning to lose its jounciness and skin tone. Only just beginning on one side, that is – the right side. The left side is strikingly fallen and prematurely aged –

like a collapsed wall or a toppled stack of books; a shift in the earth's plates; soil creep, glaciation. Flesh that has come loose from the bone and succumbed to gravitational forces. But it isn't a horror show; it gives her a specialness and presence, almost as if she has been deformed into existence.

We shook hands and settled on a day when I would come to see her, which was today.

I lifted the receiver to acknowledge the alarm call, turned over, and woke late. The Duke is the sort of hotel of course where the shower curtain billows in and clings stubbornly to your body, turning you into a turkey in shrink-wrap. I towelled down and got dressed quickly before the mirror could demist and render a full deadly accounting.

Everything was just killing time until I was due to see Veorah Batcheller at three. I still get nervous. I felt jumpy; ragged, voided of curiosity, of questions; a curiosity-free zone. I'd been hearing the Balham arrowmen or bowlers crashing around the corridors for hours, belching, farting, full of hot gas and bolshie grey-shoe bonhomie.

Outdoors, the cavalcade was as before. Mad Maxers, goths, crusties, traipsing zomboid families. Edwardian arcades with window displays unmodified since VE Day – gentlemen's cravats and sandals and ladies' steam-moulded pisspot hats; old-time cakes with deep fondant icing sitting under layers of dust. I had a hot-dog with the works, and enjoyed it so much I had another, then regretted it immediately. This was at a wooden cabin on a part of the beach where they let cars park in rows on the tawny compacted sand. Cars, dogs pissing against cars and, some way off, in the lee of the rocks, overnight encampments, fires still smouldering. The cabin looked like the shacks I saw yesterday from the train, only spruced up with a lick of blue paint and enlivened with advertising flags and pennants. 'I am terribly bored,' somebody had written on the corner of the picnic table where I was sitting, adding the time and date. In my dark business suit, my shirt and tie, I was inappropriately dressed. I could feel my collar melting, as the 'furters revolved on their griddle, and waves broke gently on the beach, and the seagulls wheeled.

Pushing '7' on the remote filled the whole screen of the television back at the hotel with the time. The second-pulsar between the two sets of digits was synchronous with the throbbing in my gut and in my head. Twenty minutes to my meeting with Veorah Batcheller. Thirteen. I read the cuts pertaining to the series of attacks at the police memorial sites squatting on the toilet. Trying to remind myself what I was doing here. Anxious to persuade myself that I could have any interest in rooting around in the reasons why somebody would make a regular round-trip of upwards of five hours to clean a memorial erected to a person she had never known. Was she a 'Nothing-says-lovin'-like-something-from-the-oven' person? Pert slogans in pokerwork? Clouded Formica? Death by trinkets? Did I care? I unwrapped two new long-life batteries, removed the used ones from the tape recorder, got confused over which was which, and headed for the toilet again. Seven minutes. I pressed 'play' and heard: 'Which do you hate more, serial killers or flab?' Who was this? When? Ten years ago? Fifteen? My own ingratiating laughter, soon to be erased by my own entirely transactional noises of care and concern.

Veorah Batcheller lives just a short walk from the hotel in a house called 'Isle of View', which sounds like, but isn't, one of the bed-and-breakfast establishments – New Moorings,

Gullsway, Lingalonga, The Bucket and Spade — by which it is surrounded and whose raucous pantomime of visual jabber shouts it down.

Right at Our Lady Star of the Sea, straight until the second set of traffic lights past the Kwik Save. I look at other people at times like this and, whatever they're doing, wherever they're going, seems preferable to the bit of business I'm embarked on. I project myself into the future by a couple of hours, and imagine I see myself coming in the opposite direction, duty discharged, the latest opinion-bites and mac-nuggets of life wisdom downloaded onto tape, my bucket full. ('I just come to work with an empty bucket. And somebody fills it up every day.' Tosser's description of the news-gathering process is one I have seen repeatedly acted out on the swarming, Petri-dish beaches of Seaton. There is an almost too literal correspondence: snotty-nosed children turning out regular, bucket-shaped buckets of sand that sometimes stand up and sometimes collapse, but are always washed away by the next tide.)

Vacancies. No vacancies. Purple bricks, yellow grouting. Black and white architrave like a set of biroed-out castellated teeth, lipstick-red awning. Old flesh sunning itself in patioed front gardens, newspapers shielding their eyes to get a good squint at the buttoned-up stranger. (Cop? Bailiff? Salesman come to ease, tease, coax and wheedle her into having one of the synthetic rough stone walls popular with the rest of the street? — walls illustrating the spectrum that pale English skin goes through towards tanning. A blowhard come to persuade her of the anti-fade advantages of getting awninged-up?)

'Isle of View'. A retiring single front squeezed in among the multi-frontages of its neighbours. A piece of industrial archeology bolted to the wall between the two upper windows: a squariel, symbol of thwarted energy and possibility; of all those project meetings and brainstorming lunches; all that booze, all those chemical assisters; all those breaking-the-mould dockos, talk shows, sit-coms still-born. Veorah Batcheller's squariel: still waiting, willing, expectant; still ready to receive but nobody available to send.

The house name was written on a ceramic tile in a wrought-iron frame at the side of the door, black letters under a palm tree standing on a cartoon desert island. One ring brought a chopped-up figure hurrying towards the reeded glass.

She was wearing an old Police tour T-shirt, the three faded peroxide heads on the front, a list of long-forgotten dates on the back. April 17th, my birthday, they played Leicester DeMontford Hall, I noticed as I followed Mrs Batcheller down a short, Haze-scented corridor and into a room where the curtains were partly drawn against the sun.

'Coffee, tea, something stronger? I've got everything in the kitchen.'

'Tea,' I said.

'Are you sure? I've only got bags or bags. Milk and sugar?'

The left, the damaged side of her face, looked no worse than if she had just been sleeping on it: Slumberland tribal scars; an aerial photograph of the Kalahari; rilled sand. A hot redness where the neck of her T-shirt had been pulled out of shape. A comma-shaped tarn under the pulled eye. She stood in the flooded wedge of light, inviting this scrutiny, not averting her face.

The television was on but muted. Two men in green and damson All England Club ties reminiscing through an unscheduled rain break at Wimbledon. Frequent cut-aways to the crowd with their macs and Teflon kagouls and colourful promotional umbrellas, waving and gagging for the camera; the tented covers over the court; the ivy-covered pavilion. Modern invented rites; the sense of life as ritual; the performance by celebrants of prescribed behaviours. Back to the talking heads in the studio, one of whom was an old-time champion I knew I should recognise behind the glasses, beyond the Tampa ennui, under the hair dye too inkily dense for his papery pale post-operative face.

The sofa was low, velour-covered, squashy: like sitting on a nursery hippo. To the left of it, the sort of heavy wooden sideboard you would get individualised cereal cartons and pitchers of grapefruit and orange juice set out on in the mornings if it was in the front room of any other house in the street. Here there was a 'still life' of driftwood and ribbons, spray-painted gold, and a framed black-and-white picture of a pop group — a 'beat combo' as they would have been referred to when the picture was taken — called, according to the name written on the bass-drum, The Guise: a four-piece in dark suits and white shirts with stand-up collars, heavy pompadours and winklepickers with caved-in, turning-up toes, which carbon-dated them as late '61/early '62.

The walls were white-on-white — 'classical', sconce-cornered panels of satinised white wallpaper set into areas of flat-painted Spanish-plaster anaglypta. It was difficult to know what they actually were because they were obscured in shadow, but drawn on pieces of paper on the sideboard wall were a series of join-the-dots rhomboids, trapezoids, tetrahedrons — like diagrams for motor-racing circuits, tournament-golf courses, airport runway systems; line charts of acupuncture points, megalithic sites, the moons of Jupiter.

The motion-detector flicked on behind its milky casing when she came in carrying the tray. She was carrying cigarettes and a lighter in one hand and she went on holding them while she poured the tea, then placed them beside her on the pillowy pitched arm of the chair. She was wearing multicoloured leggings, bright-banded like ironstone, and a ring threaded on a fine gold chain that sat dead-centre over Sting's nose.

They were still having weather in London; a slow pan from the crowd upwards through the centre-court bowl showed further rain clouds massing. Her curtains framed a cube, not much bigger than the TV screen, of brilliant blue. On the screen, yesterday's hero was still going, his hair glassy black but with a hint of tan undercolouring at the temples and neck, like a well-exercised Dobermann.

'Have you noticed you see more and more men and women with the same colour hair these days? The same colour as each other, I mean. Couples dyed out of the same bottle. It always suggests an unusual complicity, it seems to me. Active and passive. Each of them taking their turn at the sink. As if they were conspiring together in concealing something.'

Easeful, casual, apparently unscripted (actually unscripted in this case – it was one of those things you have no idea you're going to say until you've said it). Ease, tease, coax and wheedle. The rules of engagement. The age-old human dispy-doodle.

'Murderers' wives,' she said. ' "She must have known." ' She smiled a lopsided smile, pushed with her fingers against the paralysed part of her face, realigned the corners of her mouth. She brought one foot up under her. 'Hugh – Hugh was my husband – he had a thing about hair. He was obsessed with going bald. Even then' – she indicated the picture of The Guise on the sideboard – 'when he had enough for the four of them and some left over, he was always asking to borrow your mirror, always checking to see how much hair there was in his comb. He let it run rampant in the hippy era, peace, love, groovy. I used to plait it. Tie it up in bunches like a girl's, braid it with tape and coloured ribbons. It was down to here. They used to make him wear a hairnet at work, gingham nylon with a funny little visor cap attached. He didn't care.'

She brought the picture over and tapped with her nail on the lightly dusted glass to indicate which one was Hugh, although the four of them looked so much like one another it couldn't make any difference. ' "You have to know blood, you have to know diseases, you have to know everything that pertains to the human body so you can understand why hair grows," he used to say,' she said. 'He couldn't stand to watch the snooker players slowly going bald, turning into spam-heads as he called them, on the television. Footballers, newsreaders, anybody. When he finally had his long hair cut off he kept it. It's still upstairs somewhere in the carrier bag he brought it home in, I think.'

She returned the picture to its place. Then she aimed the clicker to turn off the television. The fizzling blank screen seemed to intensify the silence in the room, bring up the incidental noise of a summer afternoon beginning the long descent towards evening. With less to look at there was more to hear. The opening exchange seemed text-dragged from a place further into the conversation, relocated, reweighted on the screen. We were suddenly awkward with each other. Now it begins.

'Mrs Batcheller . . .'

'Ray,' she said. 'Mrs Ray. Ray is my married name. I went back to calling myself Batcheller after . . . ' I wanted the machine on. I should have had it on already (one-touch recording, voice-activated tape). Now it would have to wait. She was out of her chair. She roamed quietly in the room, cigarettes and lighter held at a ninety-degree angle to her body, a small clean platform under the dome of her hand, at thigh height. She stopped at the window and lifted the edge of the curtain. 'This only happened after my husband walked out on me,' she said, again pushing upwards against the left side of her face. 'I didn't believe it at first. I went to bed with a bottle of gin under my pillow. I didn't get out of bed for a week, longer. I cut off my hair and put a dark brown rinse on what was left of it. I started wearing his clothes. The only clothes he took were the clothes he was wearing. I wore his favourite shirt, his jeans, T-shirts, sweaters. I lost so much weight. Two stone in four weeks. I felt so altered as to be invisible. And then this happened. I watched it happen. I feel I saw it happen – the flesh of my face fall away like snow folding and slipping down a roof. PTSD. Post-traumatic stress disorder. I'm lucky. People have been known to become cripples, go blind. They cry for a year and when they stop they can't see. Their minds close down and then they refuse to see any more.'

Was this the cue for personal disclosure? The time to give an account of my own period in the interzone? It is a sound principle, with proven returns: hit them with your troubles and they will hit you with theirs. 'It happened in Cambodia, Vietnam,' I said. 'After the beating, or the disembowelling, or the beheading, or the hanging, or the shooting, or the incineration. People went blind from being unable to absorb the suffering and the death, things that were too powerful for them to manage or take on board. For a long time afterwards they weren't able to see anything except areas of light and dark . . . When did he leave? How long ago did it happen?'

'I want you to see something.' Instant hard-on. Into trust mode. I buttoned my jacket as I followed her next door to the kitchen, turning on the tape recorder as I went, eyes adjusting to the all-over sunshine yellow like being inside a yolk. The kitchen was oblong, spotless of course, operations centre for the buffer and scourer of monuments, its functional nature disguised by a plethora of feminine embellishments, decorations; everything regimented, replenished, colour-matched, spares standing by, nothing let to be itself. There was a rouched curtain of floral chintz, a sit-up breakfast bar, a framed print of Van Gogh's 'L'Arlésienne', a tea cosy in the shape of a marmalade cat, a mug tree, a pot pyramid with tiny tight bows attached at each level. Squeezed onto a shelf supported by human arm-shaped brackets, a collection of airport novels, some of them no doubt cranked out by hackettes of my acquaintance as a one-way ticket out of the daily deadline grind. The raised foil titles along the spines picked up the light like the lightened streaks in her hair, the pages water-warped and swelled by condensation.

She removed a half-apron from the drawer handle on which it was hanging, transferred it neatly to the back of a chair, smoothing it like a pregnant woman smoothing a dress over her stomach, and pulled the drawer open. She lifted out the knife-and-fork tray and stepped back, making room for me. In the right-hand side of the drawer were assorted oddments – an egg-slicer, a tea strainer, a nutmeg grater, the four-inch rubber seals for kilner jars. On the left side, in the upper left-hand corner, in the less-faded part where the knives and forks had been, a man's head, about two inches by an inch and a half, clipped from a magazine or newspaper, and close-cropped to eliminate background. Sparse moustache. Hooded eyes. Afro hair curling in around the edges. The see-through glueyness of old scrapbooks, of rain-lashed advertising hoardings and posters.

'Jimi Hendrix.'

'Close,' she said. 'Yes, but no.'

She went over to a tall cupboard and came back with a similar picture, this time pasted to the underside of a vacuum-cleaner head, flat against the metal, snowy and faded. I started to get the idea: sneaked communings; furtive glimpses. The same face concealed all over the kitchen, all over this house, this 'Isle of View', as in a children's puzzle-picture. She was enjoying setting this new trail, thickening her mystery. Her hair was pulled back; lifted off her neck; dampness at the hairline.

'I'll give you a clue,' she said. 'He was born in Dublin in 1951 and passed over in London in 1986. His music was hard rock with a lyrical romantic twist. A double lead sound à la Wishbone Ash.'

But I had already placed the face, come up with a name: Phil Lynott, singer with nineteen-seventies B-division also-rans, Thin Lizzy, and an unexpected object of erotic obsession, if this in fact was what she was driving at. I spun it out, curious to know where the next picture was going to come from. It came from the third Le Creuset pan down on the pyramid, and was attached to the inside of the lid – Lynott in a cowboy-style neckerchief and hooped curtain-ring ear-ring, head angled back, eyes lowered, the classic in-performance pose: guitar solo as fellatio.

'I give up,' I said. 'You've got me. I don't know.'

But she looked disappointed rather than pleased. 'I thought you might have written him up sometime. Gone to interview him. He was in the papers a lot around the time he got married. Phil Lynott, Thin Lizzy. "Killer on the Loose". You must know "The Boys Are Back in Town".' She sang some to remind me – ' "The boys are back, the boys are back in town" ' – her hands lightly fumbling (memories of all those times in front of the mirror), playing bashful airbrushed air-guitar.

'You said about the drink being in here earlier. I think I could tuck a drink away now.' She opened a corner door with the booze stacked up on it, the bottles on little fenced-in triangular shelves, tinkling, shivering. She set down two glasses and I poured two good measures of vodka, then topped them off with coke, the cloud-core ice making small encouraging explosions.

'The knife-and-fork drawer was the first place. Then I put one at the bottom of a laundry basket, behind the toilet-brush holder, under the lining-paper of my underwear drawer, in all the places a husband would never find them.' We were perched on high stools with an elbow apiece on the counter and one foot each on the floor, like wiseacres in a *New Yorker* cocktail-hour cartoon. 'I saw him first on TV,' she continued, 'and then I got to see a Thin Lizzy concert. And it became more and more an obsession with me, so that nothing else mattered but him. And I found this girl – a woman, really; she was married like I was, and even had children – she felt the same way about him as I did and we used to send each other these letters. I kept her letters locked up in a case and needless to say Hugh found it one day – I have to admit I had been behaving strangely – and broke it open. As well as the letters this girl had written to me was one I was writing to her. He never knew I was in love with Phil to that point. When he found out he said it all had to stop, that I had to pull myself together and get rid of all the pictures I'd put up. He said I could keep the records – he said the records were different, but I had to get rid of all the pictures and I wasn't allowed to keep scrap-books or anything like that. And so it went on, rows, mainly over looking at the pictures. Which is when I made the decision to put them in places where only I knew they were there. I suppose go underground with them. That was the start of the private conversations, the secret assignations over the Jif and the Toilet Duck and the dirty socks.'

'And then he rumbled you?'

'He came in here. Most of his hair gone now, just a monkish fringe at the back and sides, splaying over his collar. He came in – it was different then, a different colour. A much different layout, the cooker here where the breakfast bar is, for instance, much older appliances. The familiar sounds of him moving about. The habit he had of washing his own cup, leaving it to stand overnight on the drainer. I was sitting in the next room, turning the pages of a magazine, watching television, thinking – I don't know – whether chops or sausages, or what about fish for a change tomorrow – and he's in here with a Magic Marker writing "cancer hole" on the wall. "Cancer hole" in foot-high letters from there to there. That's what he wrote. Meaning me? My body? This house? The world? I still don't know. Then put his head around the door and said he was going out to get a part for the car. I never saw him again.'

Reality can be riveting, even for a pro. Real life. The hidden factors, the things that don't get out. Tosser was going to cream his jeans. 'He had bought a holiday for us in Lanzarote, as a surprise,' she said. 'It was going to be our first holiday together for five or six years. It was just ten days away, the outstanding balance cleared, the whole thing booked and paid for. The police sent somebody out there on the dates, just in case, to mix and mingle, standard funeral procedure, but he didn't show up.' Two people who have forgotten what it had felt like to be married and intimate with somebody, sitting talking in a kitchen, a simple two-picture.

Back in the other room she stood at the window and drew back the curtains. Something theatrical in the gesture – a gesture that is inherently theatrical – a two-arm flourish, jerking by force of habit in anticipation of the right-hand curtain snagging on its runner, serving into the sun. A dim neon glow from the leafy pattern covering the armchairs and the sofa. Micromotes coursing into the electromagnetic field of the silent television. Veorah Batcheller hit her marks. She took up a position – a posture – by the door at the end of the room's longest wall, a suggestion now of something bolstered, a stiffening, something girdled about her middle, a teacher impatient for the class to settle, waiting to begin the lesson, cigarettes and lighter still clutched in that oddly evocative way.

'Those who die violent and sudden deaths,' she began, 'nearly always have great difficulty in passing over. Many of them awake in the afterlife believing themselves still to be on Earth, and can only wander aimlessly until some form of assistance is given to them.'

The wall she was standing beside was the one that the back of my head had been staring at earlier. In the still strong afternoon light I could see that it was divided up into an elongated chequer-board pattern of black and white. The black spaces were very black, almost ebony, and were very obviously representations of the police memorials – life-size impressions obtained from charcoal rubbings of the granite skins, careful, systematic, every pimple and pore and crater, every fault and asperity faithfully rendered. The nine uniform inscriptions 'Here fell . . . ' and a date. The nine Metropolitan Police badges, engraved into the uprights. The nine gravelly patinas. These serial, repeated objects, uniform in their leathery darkness.

The white spaces with which they were twinned were as visually hectic as the rubbings were austere. They were filled or part-filled with leaves, twigs, dead flowers and miscellaneous bits of street debris – cigarette ends, Tube tickets, chocolate wrappers – whose significance wasn't immediately obvious; cumulatively, they suggested a parody or perversion of the pretty patterns – the climbing rosebuds and nasturtiums, the sunny chintz – in the kitchen.

She went on talking while I tried to absorb some of the detail, providing background on how PC X was shot here, PC Y stabbed there; telling me nothing new, nothing I didn't already know, that I hadn't already *gleaned* from disparate sources, a smoothly unspooling recitation of facts, figures, names, places.

Topophilia. Stigmataphilia. Lithomania – the human obsession with stones. The stone erected in memory of Yvonne Fletcher was a dense negative of itself: the parched white of the original here turned viscid black. The memorial to Alan King in Walthamstow was disfigured with a five-inch hole gouged out of the side, a section of the internal metal armature exposed. Two of the inscription plates had been extended to ovals to incorporate lists of three names. The stone commemorating the Harrods bombing is made of blue-veined polished Carrara marble to conform with the store's façade, and this had produced a smooth, virtually uninflected image. The upper portions of the memorials where rapes had taken place were framed or haloed with feathers, shells, pieces of evergreen.

What else? There was a picture postcard of Avalokitesvara, a fourteenth-century Japanese Buddhist deity, welcoming the souls of the dead, according to the caption (evidence of Robin Carson being round for an early sniff?). Also a jumpily typed-out quotation from the Revelation of St John: 'To those who have won the victory I will give some of the hidden meaning. I will also give each of them a white stone, on which a real name is written.'

'You travel up to London to clean the Yvonne Fletcher memorial on a regular basis,' I said. 'But all the other things you have here, the pressed flowers and bus tickets and what seem like pieces of litter and so on – does that mean at one time or another you have been to clean up all the other memorials as well? Some of them are in places where you wouldn't let your dog roam the streets on its own.' I felt the tape recorder in my pocket click off halfway through this, and by the end was aware of the heat invading my ears. I hoped she hadn't heard.

'Where in the paper are they planning to put whatever it is you have in mind to write about me? Under "freak news"?'

There was a blizzard of notation as she turned to come around the sofa, the white-on-black column of Police tour dates on her back aligning with a black-on-white list on the sideboard wall: 140 D 13, 62 D 15, 135 R 4, 29 S 11, 131 O 8, and so on, map references, an evolving method of cracking the Lottery, appliance registration numbers. 'You already know a lot about me,' she said, 'but I still don't know who you are. An overweight man in his fifties. M&S suit and socks. Vain. Bit of a drink problem. A bad sleeper, I should say. Somebody who sees the world as something removed, separate "out there". Somebody who is only happy being the surveyor of the scene but outside it, separate from what he sees. You could be a pervert, a con-artist, some shit-for-brains waiting to pull a knife on me, some psychopath who would think nothing of doing me in. A cop hater.'

'I . . .'

'No, don't tell me, I don't want to know. To be honest, I was under the impression you were somebody else at first. Norman Mailer. Whoever he is. A writer, I know, but that's all I know about him.' I was on the sofa, she was in the chair by the television, Derby and Joan who used to be Jack and Jill, both of us reinstated in our original positions. 'Desert-horror hubby, tax-tangle comic, sex-storm barmaid, plunge mum, stab dad . . . You have the power to "make" me,' she said. 'You're going to rewrite me, to boil me down for public consumption. Yvonne woman. Scrubber saint. WPC memorial angel.'

Veorah Batcheller. Veorah Ray. The Guise. Hugh Ray. 'Your husband was called Hugh. Hugh Ray? What kind of parents would do that to their son?'

'His friends called him "Tony". It's what I called him for a long time after I met him . . . People called Miller used to always get "Dusty", didn't they? Dusty Miller. Dusty Rhodes. My best friend at school's dad.' She shivered suddenly, rubbed at the gooseflesh that had sprung up on her arms. 'You know that expression that somebody's just walked over your grave? . . . What do your friends call you?'

'Norman,' I said. 'Norm, Normal, Normsky. "The Norman Mailer of the Dog and Duck". That's how I log on actually, when I've got something to put into the system at work. "N. Mailer". Although I also have a password for confidentiality that nobody else is supposed to know.'

'What is it?'

' "Fullalove".'

'Full of love?'

'One word. "Fullalove". A lot of people use the names of their children, which you're not supposed to do. Max, Leo, Alice, Jack. Today's equivalent of the school picture in the vignetted cardboard oval. In jobs where security is a priority you're issued with a list of passwords that the system bars you from using because they're too easy to guess. Jesus, Hendrix, Hitchcock, Hitler. Alka-Seltzer, Aristotle, Brando, Beatles. All car makes, movie stars, football teams, holiday destinations.'

'I know what mine would be.' A wild smile, pygmy seed pearl teeth, a lot of gum. ' "Ikkoku", which is Japanese for "pilgrimage",' she said. ' "The going out and the coming back". "A voyage in the symbolic realms of death".'

With the onset of evening, the wrinklies had retreated behind the glassed-in porchlets up and down the street, sunk deep in 1950s 'studio couches' they would have to be heaved out of when the time came, barricaded behind low tables and bottles of white salad cream and boot-brown bottles of sauce, gummily masticating, legs agape. They appeared museum-ised, Congo capuchins, grebes, preserved in vitrines.

A key plot development for them all to chew over was the fact that I was not alone. Or, rather: Veorah B wasn't setting out on her evening hike on her own as usual, but with a man – a suit – in tow, the two of them on apparently chit-chatty terms, each respecting the other's space.

Like everybody who has got used to living alone (I should know), her routine is set, her timetable inflexible. At a quarter to six she had stood up and walked out of the room as if an internal alarm had gone off. She came back a few minutes later kitted out in white trainers with pink laces and thick tongues and something bubble-like, some transparent valve or gizmo, in the heel; plus a cardigan draped over her shoulders for when it grew colder later, with a chill blowing in off the sea. It seemed to be taken as given, without anything being said by either of us, that I would be going with her on her walk.

Although it is almost ten years since her husband bailed out, she said she never ceased to be aware of the possibility that he could be alive and lurking nearby somewhere, watching, nursing his hatred of her, waiting until she drops her guard. There had been reported sightings in Denmark, Manila, Prague and Australia. The last she heard he was supposedly living in a tent and working as an evangelist on the seafront at Blackpool. She keyed in a series of codes on a digital panel in the hall before we left, activating a complex network of electric eyes, smoke detectors, sequence-timers for the lights and mortice locks.

Five minutes brought us to a litter-strewn malled area with shops specialising in beach toys and bulk-buy sweets and toffees and shabby holiday souvenirs set out in a circle around a dribbling fountain. Beyond it, at the end of a short concrete tunnel, was a harbour with blackboards advertising fishing trips and pleasure boat rides, and primary-coloured perforated metal benches set into pyramidal concrete slabs. A topless woman lay face down on a towel a few feet away from the caterpillar track of a giant dredger. The dustbins stood ankle deep in styrofoam trays and cups. Several children frolicked naked in a rancid, almost drained-dry paddling pool.

It was around here that Veorah started to put some distance between us, striding ahead on her pistoning little legs, skirting the dreck, and leading the way between bramble bushes onto a steep upward track that ran adjacent to some aggressively fenced-off back gardens but then quite soon brought us within sight of the sea. Every half-mile or so for a while, the same handwritten notice fixed to a tree. 'Lost', it said above a snapshot picture. 'Brindle bitch. Answers to "Briggie". Loving companion desperately missed. Small reward offered by pensioner owner for information leading to return.'

Blistered sea on one side. High-piled dry thorny scrub on the other. Breathless 'hi's and 'good evening's to maundering shell-suited, bum-bagged couples, desiccated outward-bounders, people wrapped in the skins of wild animals lamming off through the bracken towards stone outbuildings and cottages patched over with driftwood, cardboard, blue fertiliser bags.

When I caught up with Veorah she was doing stretching exercises on a grassy promontory that dipped gently and then collapsed precipitately in a heap of grey cuboid rubble into the sea. She was on the ground, contorted in a sort of semi-splits, trying to achieve a contact between the toe of one trainer and her head. Below us, two tiny figures were fishing off an oblique column of rock. In the deep distance, the hut where I had eaten hot dogs earlier in the day, its appearance inducing now a kind of loneliness and nostalgia that I recognised as sentimental, unearned. Power boats ripping through the old-gold.

She whipped back her hair, perspiring, blowing hard, and

lay staring at the sky. I sat down on the grass slightly behind and not quite beside her and neither of us said anything for a while. On the path above us, the occasional evening footslogger, curiosity whetted by the recumbent figures, looking and not looking, walking for the sake of walking, imprinting the dust.

'The flow of pilgrims in Mecca is counter-clockwise, against the normal passage of the sun. Whereas Buddhist pilgrims walk around their sacred stupas in a clockwise direction, along the path of least resistance, going with the flow.' There was a map of the pilgrimage route around the Buddhist temples on the Japanese island of Shikoku pinned to Veorah's living-room wall, along with maps showing Irish holy places, medieval, Marian and twentieth-century shrines.

Skellig Michael, Lough Derg, Croagh Patrick, Our Lady's Island, Knock. Awa, Tosa, Iyo, Sanuki. Fatima, Garibandal, Lourdes, Zeitoun in Cairo, Medjugorje. The Kop, Kent State, the Texas Schoolbook Depository, the Dakota building, Graceland. The place names joined with thick pencil lines to make the shapes I had at first taken to be diagrams for Formula One circuits or acupuncture points; the shapes traced and laid over one another in − I guessed − the search for correspondences, echoes, hints of synchronicity with the nine-sided, roughly kite-shaped figure you get − that Veorah had got − by linking the police memorial sites in a chain.

With the Yvonne Fletcher memorial numbered '1', reading clockwise, in chronological sequence, they went: 1, 2, 7, 3, 5, 4, 9, 6, 8. The rape sites − 5, 2, 4, 6 − were marked by coloured pins. I was certain this was where the story was − ritual, shrines, post-literate paganism, folk mysticism − and had already made a number of unsuccessful attempts to get a conversation going in this area. 'On the M25, the circular ringroad, there are fifty per cent more accidents on the clockwise carriageway than on the anti-clockwise one,' I tried again. 'You are more at risk in the autumn and least likely to be involved in an accident if you choose to go anti-clockwise in the spring.'

'My father thought this was heaven on earth,' she said, 'these few miles of the coast. He bought a plot here for next to nothing after the War, and built a cabin on it with scraps of material he brought down by bus and bicycle on his days off from work. I was born in the shack town in a black timbered house on stilts called "Perseverence" spelled wrong. It was like growing up in the Wild West.' The heat of the day radiating from the hard packed earth at twilight. She gathered a bunch of tiny, garnet-coloured flowers where she was sitting and put them in one of the button-holes of her cardigan.

We walked on for a while, in single file because of the narrowness of the path, until we came to some candles in coloured glass bottles planted in the earth. There was an offertory box for donations towards a more permanent memorial to the local woman who, a plaque explained, had been murdered at this spot almost exactly a year earlier while walking her dogs. There were bunches of flowers, a jade plant in a pot, a card printed on chlorine-free board from a renewable source, placed there by the woman's son: 'I used to watch you so intently when I was a baby and a toddler, I studied your every move. I wish I could say "See you soon." Your son ———'.

A light flickered in a cylinder jar with Martin Luther King's 'I have a dream' speech printed on it, the last few lines disappearing into the ground.

We took the circular route back to Seaton, following dimming lanes to a farming hamlet where the shadow show against the windows of the only pub easily reeled us in.

The Stand Alone was white-painted, broad-walled, erratically added-onto, thatched — and stood alone in the fork between two unlit roads, still little more than tracks. The apple-knocker rusticity extended inside, where the ceilings were low, smoky, concussively beamed, the walls bedizened with bridles, ferrets and weasels in cases, rods and reels, fishing flies mounted and framed. All of it, it became clear pretty quickly, by-the-yard and brewery supplied.

'Bottle of Diamond White, tin of Tennents Super, packet of kingsize Rizla red.' The first order I overheard indicated how far we were from the bought-in Isaak Walton idyll represented on the walls. The buyer was Elvisly coiffed, tattooed, female, slightly boss-eyed, part of a big group of bikers and their coozes who were the audience for an old yokel who was taking bets on two live crabs he was trying to get to race each other across the floor. 'Prostitution, Alcoholism, Serious Substance Abuse but, above all, a really wonderful atmosphere', a sign announced behind the bar.

We stood as far away from the crab Olympics as possible, which wasn't far enough to stop the terrible smell of the old man mugging us every so often as he stumbled around, flapping his arms, trying to get the half-dead crawlers to put a spurt on. The bikers flicked cigarette-ends and burning matches at them, and doused them with Tennents and mad cider sprayed between their teeth.

We were asked to move after a few minutes — shift our shanks — so that a ladies' dart match could begin, the darters each with a fag going in their throwing hand, a floret of brown mole nestled in the sparse underarm hair. Nasal redneck music, a small digital display running a repeating repertoire of jokes: 'Joke,' it flashed. 'Joke ... What's small, red and sticky? ... Answer: A baby with a razor blade.' The stutter smear of dot-matrixed laughing mouths.

When was it I gave him the matches? – the half-full box from the White Tower, Fitzrovia's finest, with which he was going to immolate himself. I can see it all now, of course: the open fire in his hovel, the crossed planks resting on the wooden crate, inched in slowly as they burned, the water to be brought to a boil for the crabs, the thunderous blowback when he poured the paraffin on ... Oh I can see it vividly now. But I couldn't see it then, when I made him a present of the matches to get rid of the spectacular smell, and was vaguely aware of him scrambling together his crabs (which he had tried to sell us) and lurching out into the night.

He lived only a matter of feet away as it happened, stumbling distance, in a terraced cottage whose front door opened straight into the road, and where I was next to see him, hair, beard and flesh aflame, listing slowly sideways on his sofa, turning into crackling, like the picture of the Buddhist monk Thich Quang Duc who flambéd himself in the Saigon market in the early years of the war. ('If only Heath was here,' was my first thought. 'This would go *bosh*! ... right in the paper. As it is – four pars in the local free sheet, six pars max.')

I've covered air crashes and therefore know what burning flesh smells like. It smells sickly sweet like pork, but acrid as well, like when you burn a saucepan and there's that harsh bit that lodges in your throat. First, though, there was the smoke belching round the door, then the flames when some-body from the pub bolted out and stove the windows in. The rush to witness wasn't immediate, or even total. The music kept playing (the pub looking starship-like in the still blue night), the visual display kept putting up its jokes.

There was a strange uncomfortable hiatus between the realisation of what was happening and the arrival of the emergency services on the scene. We stood in the summer light-rimmed dark, the fire taking a hold, trying on appropriate expressions, working up suitably laconic versions of the drama, denying the life charge, the excitement. And then the loudest, the most foul-mouthed (it would have to be) of the bikers, the one in the ripped Korean bomber jacket with the pouncing tiger on the back, started plainly, without a smirk, growing in resonance as other rumbling voices joined in: '*The Lord is my shepherd, therefore can I lack nothing. He shall feed me in a green pasture and lead me forth beside the waters of comfort. He shall convert my soul and bring me forth in the paths of righteousness for his Name's sake. Yea, though I walk through the valley of the shadow of death I will fear no evil for thou art with me; thy rod and thy staff comfort me. Thou shalt prepare a table before me in the presence of them that trouble me; thou hast anointed my head with oil and my cup shall be full. Surely thy loving-kindness and mercy shall follow me all the days of my life and I will dwell in the house of the Lord for ever.*'

'Amen,' the congregation said.

'Amen,' I said.

'Amen,' said Veorah Batcheller, who took the garnet-coloured flowers she had gathered earlier and placed them at the dead man's charred door.

'How did that happen?' We were walking between high deeply concave dark hedges, a strong impression of the sea somewhere off to the left, completing our round-trip to Seaton. Shoulder to shoulder in the uncertain light. 'Because you were there,' she said. One foot in front of the other; breathing out and breathing in.

'He was going to do it anyway, but you being there made it happen faster. Something in your personality, can I say aura, made it happen. You recognise the possibility of something happening, a man who functions in excitements other people create, and so it does. It's sort of like sex. Some people give off sex and other people respond. It's the same thing with madness or violence or whatever else. It's in the air; it's given off by certain people. You're more like a medium. You give permission. You're like an enabling factor.'

We parted at a municipal square on the promenade, Roman in intention, built as a spectacle, now semi-derelict, let go, people sleeping on the benches and in the shelters. I kissed her on the melted cheek and met living tissue rather than an advance outpost of death, a reminder of the death that is ensconced in the body, the first part of her to die.

The dog is doing nothing to let me down, showing gratifying signs of wear and tear, getting to look as dirty as a rag. I had agreed an extension with the hotel to six o'clock, which is how long this hit and run was going to take me: three hours tops. But it was after ten, my room had been given to somebody else and my travelling companion, my potchke, my fleutchke, my notchke, my motchke, was dumped nose-down on the top of my bag behind the desk in Reception, looking abject – orphaned and evicted.

But a few phone calls and a tenner in the right place got us this crib in an identical establishment down to the cock-neys and the cooking smells a hundred yards further along the street.

I have been lying here for hours letting all of the above,

Rohypnol or no Rohypnol, work through me, pelt past me, keeping me awake. Studying the curvature of the ceiling, mentally demolishing modern flushed surfaces, partitions, stripping the room back through its earlier incarnations, lying under only the top-sheet, thinking: Isle of View Isle of View Isle of View.

Until a few minutes ago I got it. Simple. Isle of View. I love you.

I know too much. She has complicated herself beyond grasping. I know this much: I don't know where to begin.

S : I : X

Day 28. The noises from the other side of the wall that used to shock me awake, locked rigid, nerves peeled, have long since stopped. Have been stopped, I would suppose, for years. Doors slamming in the middle of the night, giggling, a booming bass, and then the sounds of slow, spirit-logged, smoke-in-the-hair, pre-dawn fucking. But I go on making my bed on the sofa in the living room anyway.

The choice to me seems simple: staying in the world, close to the safe comforts of the telephone, the television, the mini-fridge switching through its simple programme, the random acned array of electric indicator lights; or retreating to the back of the cave that the bedroom represents. The life and clutter of the one room standing in stark contrast to the inertness and passivity of the other. A dressing-table, a bed, a bedside table, a wardrobe. On the bedside table a stopped clock, by the bed a beaten pair of leather slippers. The bed stripped back to the mattress, level, bier-like, under the plain faded coverlet. A room to be gazed at rather than inhabited, registering an absence of human spirit; a room with a suspended, tableau look, petrified, Pompeian, the sense of having intruded on a domestic scene not long abandoned. (A city in the volcano, houses under the ash, skeletons in the houses, furniture and pictures next to the skeletons.)

And me putting my clothes on in there every morning a joyless ritual performed on an almost bare stage.

Few people meeting me now for the first time would have me down as somebody whose tastes once ran to clothes that made a positive, even attention-grabbing, statement about who I was and where I saw myself in the world. But it's true: I was a snappy dresser; clothes were an issue in my life. I dressed – so of course I like to think – with some *esprit* and *élan*. But then middle age grew over me like a thick skin on a custard. I physically thickened, my waist pushed yeastily up into the forties, my face became fatted with blanding prosthetic latex layers, the unclouded, undefeated me still gasping for air in there somewhere.

For some time I worked hard at persuading myself that the process was reversible; that it was something that could be turned in the opposite direction once I had recovered some kind of equilibrium; when my life had been hauled out of the ditch and made roadworthy again. Doesn't happen.

I have stayed unindividuated, neutral, absorbed into the beige mass of the everyday walking wounded. I threw away foolish things – the suit from Tommy Nutter with the wasp waist and flared lapels, the Norfolk jacket made of burgundy velour, the look-at-me Mr Fish tie – and started to dress in accordance with my new status as a non-combatant. This has meant things picked up in the covered markets and shopping precincts and high streets of draughty small towns, where I have found myself with time to kill. (So much time to kill.)

The blue, the brown, the checked, the striped, the double-breasted, the zippered, the corduroy, the cotton; the one with the top button missing, the one with the fraying cuff, the one with the grease stain that never quite comes out.

My life's tatters, systematically sorted through and arranged on hangers on Sunday evenings, six hangers, six outfits, jacket, trousers, shirt, tie, an outfit for every day of the week: six alternative, inoffensive, pre-prepared presentations of the self. Six etoliated – six *vaporised* – Norman Millers coffined in a monumental wardrobe of walnut wood veneer.

The view from the bedroom window is across stunted narrow gardens to the backs of the houses one street over. Two floors down and diagonally opposite is the window of a woman who operates what a small sign by her bell describes as a chiropody 'studio', and on some mornings – this morning was one – while I'm putting my clothes on, I watch her moving in on the disembodied white foot in the DaRay halogen white light, light that is purposeful; and clinical, fiercely non-domestic; the professional intimacy of the light-flooded foot against the nylon-sheathed thigh, the overall pulled tight across the muscular buttocks, her scalpel hand working swiftly, industriously, shredding the calluses and verrucas, stripping away the ravages of time and labour; the dead cells, the particles of necrotic tissue spinning ecstatically in the light, like an upturned snowstorm paperweight.

If it's Thursday it must be the blue polka-dot-pattern tie and the charcoal jacket. Conversely (and much more usefully), if it's the blue polka-dot-pattern tie and the charcoal jacket, it must be Thursday. The times beyond counting when it has got to that time of the day and a glance down at the colours rolling over the hump of my stomach has steadied me and given me a bearing; a hand-hold on the tilted deck, a fixed point in the churning chaos.

It is a trick that wouldn't work for me today though, because today my neckwear is of the mourning variety, glummest black, in honour of a former colleague, Curtis

Preece, just thirty and everything to play for, who is lying twenty-five feet away from me in a cedar casket, under a single tasteful cross of Arum lilies, before the altar of the church known as the 'Printers' Cathedral', St Brides.

Curtis had come to the notice of Howie Dosson when he interviewed him, and many other prominent media figures, for his university magazine. He was on an instant upmove that left Sebastian-Dominic, to name one, looking as if he had never got out of the traps. Curtis made his name breaking the story of the Cabinet Minister discovered dining naked with three boys in chorister drag, had quickly become a familiar face on late-night television, and was already being spoken of as editor material. He had in fact just been appointed launch editor of a new through-colour, youth-oriented Saturday supplement ('A *Nova* for the nineties') when, a week ago, he removed his shoes, folded his jacket neatly on top of them on the platform, and jumped in front of a west-bound District Line train.

The original driver spotted him and braked in time, but he walked on into a tunnel, waited at a bend, and then threw himself in front of a train where the driver had no chance to stop. It turned out he had left a single-line streamer message scrolling right to left across the screen of his terminal at the paper: 'Perhaps you've confused me with someone who gives a shit.' Seamlessly repeated, white on infinite blue, half-bumper sticker, half-suicide note.

The choir are singing something that, even inside their freakish blizzard of human noise, doesn't sound like a hymn:

> What have I got
> That makes you want to love me?
> Is it my body?

Or someone I might be?
Something inside me?
You better tell me. Tell me.
It's really up to you.
Have you got the time to find out
Who I really am?

The order of service says that this is a song by Alice Cooper, although it is hard to believe. Printed below the lyric, for some reason, is Curtis Preece's favourite recipe for mango chutney.

'Brace yourself for the choir, man. They'll cut your face off. They're really loud,' Heath had said when I was accosted by him on the way in. He was crouched behind a part of the graveyard wall at St Brides that gave him the cover he needed to snatch 'gut shots' of the brass of both papers as they were decanted from their Jags and Daimlers and Audis, the doors mock-deferentially held open for them by chapel fathers redunded from the print, bung artists, squarers, recidivists in vaulted mirror-peaked chauffeurs' caps.

He was especially keen to get the proprietor and, more particularly, his *consiglieri* in their thousand-guinea winter-weight suits, recurring archetypal figures down the ages, whispering in the doge's ear, drafting designs for the king's gardens, official astrologers to the czar. Slipping from the in-car, air-conditioned environment to the cool, candle-lit interior of the church, moving swiftly yet unhurriedly through the humidity and grit. A scene from a film by Roberto Rossellini – or do I mean Vittorio de Sica? – black and white, made on odds and ends of stock in the years straight after the War, ordinary people as actors.

The women are dowdied down, in keeping with the occasion. The men, though, seem pumped up, enlarged, ready to take on the beast in the jungle, should it spring out at them, and wrestle it to the ground. (A further, not-altogether-gratuitous cultural allusion, here. Minnie Kidd, Henry James's maid, said she heard the Master on his death-bed shout out: 'It's the beast in the jungle, and it's sprung,' one of the most frightening things I have ever heard.)

Tosser and Ronnie Duncan arrived in separate cars wear-ing similar alumicron suits, solid-coloured at a distance but dissolving into tiny nailhead patterns, like billboard-scale posters, when you come close. Both wearing photo-grey tinted lenses and shirts with spring-metal stays in the collars; both reflecting the razor-edged geometry and hard bright colours of the new newspaper building, unrecognisable for the rumpled, crotch-at-the-knee slobs they were just a year ago.

Pacing up and down outside St Brides was Peter Conmee, taking alternate gasps on a kingsize cancer-stick and the nozzle of his Medihaler. Conmee, once a respected foreign editor, now given the job of vetting expenses, functions on half a lung. Even smokes in the shower, so legend has it, with the aid of a small umbrella contraption he has rigged up. Sarky remarks from people going in that he was unable to hear over the noise of his hawking up catarrh and his rattling cough.

'I'd just stay here if I was you, old lad.'

' "Take my breath away, awaaay." '

'I see you're wearing Players today, Pete.'

Curtis Preece's mother, the Anna Magnani figure, arrived escorted by Clit Carson, Clit in a floating, asymmetrically cut, wraparound black kimono affair. The Tube train driver is here in the wheelchair he has been confined to since the accident. Ashley Cann and Annie Jeffers, it seems, have entered into some kind of life-swap and come as each other: he now wears a nose bolt and has moonlight-blond hair – platinum with the blue roots showing; her tufted, savagely cut hair is aubergine purple.

A sprinkling of Garrick Club ties; one Garrick Club bow-tie; the candlelight reflected in big chrome-rimmed bi-focals, old-maidish half-lenses with clear plastic, fun-coloured, tortoiseshell frames, several on retaining chains; standard blow-dries; silver hair cut quite wavy and long; red-faced men turning into toby-jug versions of their younger selves. A sudden choked-back sob; Clit's fingers intertwining with the mother's.

Ronnie Duncan steps up to the lectern to deliver the Address. 'St Augustine was once asked where time came from.' Fingers white-knuckled around the carved oak, arms tensed as if at the top of an up-push of his morning Canadian Airforce workout. 'He said it came out of the future which didn't exist yet, into the present that had no duration, and went into the past which had ceased to exist. "Man must endure his going hence even as his coming hither . . . " '

Tosser is irritably consulting his watch, scribbling memos to himself on the cuff of his shirt. 'All of us gathered here this morning who had the good fortune to know Curtis will agree with me that he conformed as close as any of us to the heroic image of the journalist defending the truth against the many dragons of darkness in the modern world . . . '

Myc Doohan, in the pew in front, is wrestling with a fistful of Jack and Jills, transferring the totals, plus service, to a swindle sheet; doing slow-brained calculations on a piece of scrap paper. '. . . his death is yet a further tragic reminder that, in a world that is so fast, so unnatural, and so attractive, we all of us spend too much time human doing and not enough time human being . . . ' (Evidence of the hand of Robin Carson. Barely suppressed groans.)

The body (suspiciously light) is carried out to the choir singing 'The Old Rugged Cross', and borne off to a marble orchard in far north London trailed by a single carful of mourners.

As soon as it has gone there is a wild scramble into the cars, a race for taxis, the slightly druggy pace of fifteen frames a second wammied into fast-forward mode; out of the forties black-and-white shadows into sun-splashed no-grain Ciba-chrome. A dramatic exodus; a fleeing from a world now occupied by the usurpers of insurance, banking, commodities speculation; the familiar turned on its former owners, inducing feelings of sadness and dread; a world changed beyond all reckoning, the field of ruins.

Behind the stained façade of the old *Express* building, stockades of desks, telephones heaped like bones; the desk where I wanked away my promise every day for four years, the phone on which I had my first conversation with Even.

The tiered white wedding-cake spire of St Brides floats on the *Express*'s black deco curtain wall, gridded and frac-tured, like a deeply moulded shaft of light; like the spook they are all fleeing.

The *Express* building, popularly known as the Black Lubi-anka. Wren's tallest spire rejoicing in the description 'a mad-rigal in stone'.

In the brochurised version, the architect had a special tunnel excavated for the convenience of the stonemasons working on his masterpiece, invisibly connecting St Brides with the Old Bell. The cut or ginnel or alley that exists today is authentically lichen-walled and burrow-like, the rotting bases of the iron posts at eye-level, the wall of the crypt rising to above-head height.

Once at this time in the morning you could have expected the Bell to be heaving. But there's hardly anybody in except Doohan and Ashley Cann.

' "The whole country watched the agonised care of the eight guardsmen who carried the box. And vicariously shared their anxious pain. But perhaps most marvellous was the slow move up the turgid Thames. There were things like the gantries of cranes dipping in salute and the music of a host of pipers. There were generals in improbable uniforms and what looked like all the rulers of the world standing on the steps of St Paul's as if this were a family burial. A whole city looking in on itself as a dead body went by." '

I recognise this. It's the piece Patrick O'Donovan did for the *Observer* on Churchill's funeral, probably five years before Ashley was born. It is my duty now – I owe it to Myc – to step in and stop him before he gets on to the wit that flew among O'Donovan and his crowd (Anthony Sampson, Terry Kilmartin, Maurice Richardson) at Philip Hope-Wallace's table in the back room at El Vino in the fifties.

'What's up Myc?' Doohan is looking glum, sitting nursing a tepid diet-Pepsi. 'You look like you've just been to a funeral. You've got a face like a toilet seat.'

'What it is,' Myc says, 'is I know there's a reason, but I can't remember why I won't talk to that cunt over there.'

Ashley laughs, but he is still off rummaging in the document folder he has accessed in his brain. 'Did either of you two ever know Ian Mackay, the *News Chronicle* columnist who spurned all efforts to lure him away from the paper he loved?' We avoid each other's glances, shuffle, shake our heads. 'Ian had asked for his ashes to be scattered in Lincoln's Inn Fields. So, after his funeral a party of his closest friends adjourned to the King and Keys with the ashes in a shoe box to talk it over. They then moved to the Punch, the Falstaff, and finally the Press Club, still in possession of the box. Over drinks they decided to scatter the ashes on the Thames near Cleopatra's Needle. But when they got to the Embankment the box was empty – it had a hole in it. They returned to the Club and consoled themselves with the thought that they had left a little of him in all the places he loved best. Boom-boom.'

What do we look like? Three white shirts, three black ties. The Guise on a remember-when seaside reunion tour with an erratic young pick-up drummer who would rather be with the Beastie Boys. 'Did you hear the one about the Murdoch henchman in Australia,' Myc says, still on the subject of death stories, 'whose wife slipped his American Express platinum card into his pocket as she bent over the coffin to kiss him goodbye, *just in case*. I should be so lucky. I'm struggling to hang on to my VAT rating as it is. It's a status requirement these days, like *von*-something used to be. Baronial. If you're not registered, they'll grind you down.'

'Is it enough to earn your age? You know what I'm saying,' Ashley says. '£27,000 a year at twenty-seven.'

'Your *age*. I tell you, I'm lucky to earn my shoe size. You can laugh,' Myc says, 'but I'm not joking . . . Anyway, what's the score with you and Annie Jeffers? The barnet and the whole bit.'

Ashley colours, then presses his hands against his face, slowly squeegeeing the blood up into the sooty roots of his two-tone hair.

All around us in the Bell are apothegms, injunctions and

motivating slogans that hung in the newsrooms of the Street, ancient and modern. 'Impact! Get it in your first paragraph! Get it in your pictures! Above all get it in your headlines!' 'Explain, simplify, clarify!' 'The public is habitual and needs the same news in the same place day after day.' 'The public is interested in just three things: blood, money, and the female organ of sexual intercourse.' 'Everybody feeds off everybody.' 'Never lose your sense of the superficial.' 'Make it first, make it fast, make it accurate. Then' (this scribbled across the bottom of the original, but retained in the interest of period resonance) 'go and make it up.'

Ashley, as usual, is wearing a lithoed or rubber-appliquéd T-shirt under his shirt, which has the effect of making his body look as though it has been imprinted with furtive, barely decipherable messages and logos – 'Metallica', 'Kick Butt', 'Youthanasia', 'Zodiac Mindwarp', 'Back the fuck up'. Subtexts. Undercodes. The fetish tattoos of a Japanese yakuza, a junior mafioso from the Roppongi club scene. All public spaces resounding with the perpetual bull-session, slogan to slogan, in which ordinary, across-the-table conversation can seem like a banal interruption of the one-worders, the one-liners, the corporate zingers. 'Phalcon'. 'Skism'. 'Gno-mist'. 'Nike Jordan'. 'The beautiful game'. 'You're just a wave, babe, you're not the water.'

'The individual is overwhelmed by an incomprehensible flood of signs, surfaces and space,' Ashley says in a time-to-hit-the-hay-old-timer sort of way when I blurt some of this out. Happy-trails. 'The sensuality of information takes over, grainy, hydra-like, pimply, pocky, ramified, seaweedy, strange, tangled, tortuous, wiggly, wispy, wrinkled. We live in an inebriated state of consciousness. Which is why we need the murderers. Murder, rape, natural disaster, atrocity stories on a daily basis.' The opening bars of the theme to *Match of the Day* play on a video football game. Another game, occasionally overlapping, jangles a snatch of the *EastEnders* theme.

'There is a community need,' Ashley continues. 'We need perpetrators. We need victims. These people *create* community. *Communitas.* By giving us stories that we can run with, that penetrate the din. The patterns and structures of stories work towards cultural cohesion. Community is in part built on members sharing the same stories. Which is where the reporters of the stories, the venerable tradition of journalism, the spinners of folk tales, come in. You, Myc, you ... Hey,' Ashley breaks off suddenly. 'Heath Hawkins – come on down!'

'Oh wonderful, wonderful, and most wonderful!' Heath says, flinging himself across a bench seat. 'And yet again wonderful, and after that, out of all whooping!' He peels off the black V-neck sweater he has on. There is a colour reproduction of the stars and stripes on *his* T-shirt. Above it, the semi-washed-out slogan: 'Try burning this one ... ', and below it, the single word: 'ASSHOLE'. He has a Smiley patch over a hole in the knee of his jeans.

'Living large, man. Living *very* large,' Heath says, replying to a question that none of us has asked. 'Did you see those ill fuckers out there? Was that bad news at the wax museum, or what? Forget Rwanda, man. Namibia, Angola, Israel, Palestine. The Hashemites, the hereditary guardians of the holy places for over a thousand years, given the order of the boot by the Saudis. These shitehawks in suits, old Tosser and his cohorts. These are the uprooted, the lost peoples, the dispossessed. Scuttling back to their glass eyries, the dickless work stations, the sealed airless rooms, the gorgon at the desk. The deterritorialised workforce. Dead white males.'

Curtis Preece ex-ed himself off-peak at Blackfriars station, about two hundred yards from where we are sitting, which is nowhere he should have been. 'You run fast, you smell bad,' Hawkins says. 'End of story. That should be carved in granite on that guy's grave. Tell you what, he certainly smells bad now, boy. Had to scrape him up, according to sources in the necropolitan underworld. One double bacon-cheese-burger, *very* rare, hold the mayonnaise.'

'The Dutch have a new word for it. The Dutch always have a new word for it,' Ashley says. ' "Zelf-doding". Which means "self-deathing", as opposed to "self-killing", which is what suicide translates as.' He has knotted the black tie around his upper arm, Comanche-fashion, using his teeth to secure the knot like a smack-head in an art-house under-ground movie of the sixties, school of Andy Warhol, Andy's children, street trash apotheosised.

'Did you hear about the death's head?' Ashley says. 'Curtis claimed that a shrieking death's head had started to appear occasionally at the top of his screen. And he wasn't alone. Quite a few people think they've seen the same thing. Hold down the option key, hit the shift key three times, your computer makes this funny trilling sound and an object appears at the corner of the screen that could, if you were sufficiently paranoid, look like a death's head. It's not a virus or a worm or anything to get hot and sweaty about. It's just a weird software thing. I tried to convince Curtis of this more than once. I even demonstrated it to him. But he was sufficiently paranoid. He was beyond convincing.'

Persistent eye, nose and throat irritation; skin rashes,

nausea, lassitude, breathing discomfort, dull but unrelenting pain in the hands and arms ... Panic attacks, morbidity, claustrophobia, a whole shitstorm of anxiety neuroses and phobic states ... This just about covers the spectrum of complaints in the year since we have been taken off the tit and shunted out to the place none of us has yet got used to calling Merry Hill Newsplex Plaza. (Packages will reach us if addressed simply to 'Merry Hell'.)

The cabling and ducting, the heating, cooling, lighting, plumbing and sewage systems all came on-site factory-fresh, and went in clean and true and apparently uninfected. How do I know? I know because, almost from day one, I was there, in hard-hat and gumboots, shadowing Owen Allen of Boyd Allen and Partners up ladders and down into the thin black slurry of the foundations of the fast-food, design-and-build khazi whose progress it was my penance to cover for the benefit of shareholders, in the annual company report.

Owen Allen is a hack who believes that cricket boots and strident striped cricket blazers teamed with designer face furniture all year round disguises the fact. The simplest description of the development he came up with would probably be 'Disnoid' – a bit of mirror-Gothic here, some imitation palazzo there, a Renaissance portico somewhere else; interior cobblestone walks, five-storey sheet fountains, 'period' carriage lamps. Standard, off-the-peg decorated shed.

But in the course of regular visits, over a period of about two years, I had to listen to his horse manure about 'the symbolic interpenetration of nature and culture' and 'the grammar of layered planes'; references to Mayan temples of sacrifice, the raked pebble garden of Ryoanji, and English eighteenth-century crinkle-crankle walls. I had to look interested while he bored on about circumstantial distortions, expedient devices, eventful exceptions, exceptional diagonals, superadjacency, equivalence, and pretend I was getting it all down. We were witnessing the rise of a building which made the workplace an aesthetically charged location. Under the polished surfaces, meanwhile, filth accrued.

Fungal spores and pathogenic bacteria incubating in the air intakes, filter traps and water tanks. The building as a lumbering, limping animal, a failing organism, with which none of us needed any encouragement to identify. Tubular organs obstructed, metabolic processes inhibited, blood vessels eroded, vital centres destroyed, biochemical balances deranged . . .

I can quote Sir Arthur Palgrave here with no fear of it being blue-pencilled, as it was in my final report: 'Coeval with the first pulsation, when the fibres quiver, and the organs quicken into vitality, is the germ of death. Before our members are fashioned, is the narrow grave dug in which they are to be entombed.' Bioslime, bioviruses, mould-spores, baffle-jelly infesting the building even as it was going up. When it was up, one of the nifty touches of the architects (that glass counterpart of the crinkle-crankle wall, a serpentine curve) meant that you risked being blinded or fried alive at your desk.

The site was a former swimming bath, public baths and wash-house, separated by a red route road from one of the toughest council estates in London. Fact: homes produce far more sewage than office buildings of roughly the same size – mountains of mucilage, cataracts of cack. And it is this, the contents of the storm drains, sewers and soil pipes, that seems to get drawn up into the building in a way nobody has been able to satisfactorily explain yet, making it smell sometimes like a tannery or slaughterhouse; a public lavatory in Madrid or the suburbs of Moscow. Uninvited bilge inching through the pipes; scum from the plunge baths and slipper baths of pre-history, a broth of matted hair and sloughed-off cells seeping into the system.

Still in the Ding-Dong, it is Myc who is speaking. 'Did you know that one in three of all old women living on their own are found to have cat food down their knickers when they're brought into hospital?'

'Is it in tins?' Ashley says.

'Klit-E-Kat.' Heath raises the biggest laugh.

'Hang on a minute,' Myc says. 'No, bag your faces. Is that my coat ringing?' His mobile is in his jacket, hanging near the door. 'How would I have heard, I'm in a meeting,' he says into the deviant-looking buckled-down black plastic sheath. 'When did this happen?' Indicating for us to keep the noise down with his hand. 'Got it . . . Got it . . . Okay . . . I'll get flying. I'm already there . . . A snap story,' he says, dipping the instrument of torture in his inside pocket, aiming himself at the door. 'Some dipshit maniac has gone on the rampage among the McGovern faithful at the hospital. They're saying two stiffed so far, a cutter job, loads of claret . . . Further misfortunes unfold.'

Ashley has gone into his computer, which has responded with a soft but insistent *bong*-ing sound, and a citron pulse which is projected with the rest of the contents of the screen across the contours of his face.

A couple of days after Curtis Preece killed himself, his girlfriend came into the office to enact a private ritual which involved sitting in his chair, handling his things, hugging everything which might have come into contact with him.

She asked to have the last words keyed into it brought up onto his screen, and she leaned in close, bathing her face in the area of ozone emission, the text and graphic display suffusing her upturned face, the field around the screen taking her long, fine hair and drawing it to itself.

She laid a single rose along the upper edge of the portrait of Curtis that is hanging by the cash dispenser at the entrance to the men's toilets. On her way out, she threw a coin into the fountain in the main reception. The basin of the fountain is always scaled with coins, but it was the first time I had ever seen anybody do this.

I was hoping to beg a lift to St Saviour's from Heath Hawkins, but he has gone, legged it.

'Life's a bitch, and then they freeze your head,' Mick says.

'Life's a bitch, and then you turn into one,' Ashley says.

The magnetic field of my animal instincts.

S : E : V : E : N

In the post this morning, a letter from Veorah Batcheller. (I had given her my home address, which is something I have hardly ever done. The phone here is ex-directory.)

Dear Norman –
    You probably think there's nothing worse than having to listen to somebody's dreams and there I agree with you. But I feel the need to tell somebody – somebody who knew me in my previous life even if slightly, before I set out on this adventure – I want to describe a dream I keep having over and over these nights.
    It's a dream about Shane Norwood, who as you will know is the son of Sean Norwood somebody I have never given any great thought to before, I have been able to take or leave him.
    Shane I'm guessing would be a young teenager somewhere around thirteen or fourteen now if he's still alive. *I am convinced that he is.* In the dream it is always the same basement or cellar area where the boy is being held – *still* after all these years. To start with it is always the same hammer horror film stuff and I want to wake up, open my eyes and run away. I am aware of feeling this even while sleeping (maybe it's the odd circumstances I get my head down in these days – the back of a black taxi in a lockup garage in Muswell Hill for example last night).
    A wobbly camera shows a man's feet going down a

flight of lion [lino] covered stairs, old fashioned open
toe style sandals, cheap nasty patterned socks. Down into
the darkness with a hint of light from a narrow transom
window at one end. You can see dead brown grass
through the window, an empty blouse hanging on a
clothesline swinging in a breeze. Another clothesline
stretches across the corner at the far end of the room.
A bucket and mop stand outside a cupboard door. A beat
up sofa against one wall. A few chairs one of them
turned upside down with the brown webbing showing.
On the left is a smaller room where you might expect
the washer and dryer to be. The walls are thick with
padded insulation. A cheap kitchen chair is positioned
in the centre of the room with a white bed sheet spread
out under the chair and now we see Shane Norwood
handcuffed and tethered to it. His knees are forced wide
apart so he straddles the chair each leg bent back at the
knee and his feet tied with the rope to the back chair
legs. Swastikas have been carved on his arms and into
his head and face. You assume at this point that some
other horrible thing is about to be inflicted on him but
what happens then is this. You see that the man who is
holding him has brought a portable television with him
down the stairs – a Sony Trinitron as it happens dirty
white with a circular aireel which he stands on the floor
by the door and plugs in. It is a few minutes before half
past 3 and the end of Sean Norwood's show when the
contestants wave at the big allumined picture and together
shout Bye Shane.

Shane raises his chin from his chest and parts his poor
dry lips to talk. Bye he whispers and there is a small
lurch as he tries to move one of his hands which are
secured behind his back to wave. The tears well up and
career if this is the word I'm looking for down his face.
But – *But* – his abductor the man who snatched him
from the bosom of his family is crying as well. And we
see that this is meant – real big hot hopeless tears.

This as I say is a dream I have been having nearly every
night. And my sense my intuition is that what happens

in the dream also happens just like this on a regular without fail basis wherever Shane Norwood is being held. Which only proves I suppose that cheap sentimental gestures – like the valentine card, the pop song, no doubt some people would say my memorial work and the course of action on which I am now currently embarked – have a place. This showbusiness thing done for whatever motives is touching his life connecting him with the world and helping Shane to survive.

I have a feeling I have been snowing you under with bits quoted from books (I have been in a kind of reading fever looking for ways to explain myself to myself and why I'm doing what I'm doing) but here is another one – A great city is a kind of labyrinth within which at every moment of the day the most hidden wishes of every human being are performed by people who devote their whole existence to this and nothing else. The hidden life of forbidden wishes exists in extravagant nakedness behind mazes of walls.

Although it plays no part in what I originally set out to do my conviction now is that somewhere along the path I have set myself is the room where Shane Norwood is tied and tethered. I know you are a sceptic – a world class cynic – and that you have to be if you want to stay in your job but I feel I am coming closer to that room every day I keep walking swept along in the flow of ordinary daily life. If you think I haven't totally gone berserkers and feel like catching up you will probably find me (see the map I sent you) at M9 – Higham Hill Rd near the junction with Mayfield Rd in Walthamstow East 17 – around tea-time tomorrow (Thursday). Perhaps I will see you then.

Best wishes,
Veorah

The piece I did on Veorah Batcheller hasn't yet made it into the paper, for a variety of reasons. The rapist seems to have peaked at four – there have been no further attacks in the vicinity of the police memorials for about two months, and so interest has cooled. Then the butchering of the fans camped outside St Saviour's (a former boyfriend of one of the women, armed to the teeth with cleavers and kitchen knives, was arrested at the scene) has been getting maximum play. Crucially, though, the editor decided my piece on Veorah sucked.

'If this is a story, my cock's a bloater,' is what he actually said as he slung the galley-proof across his desk at me, adding that he wanted it whammed up. '*Well* whammed up. The kiss of fuckin' life. Like: get off the bed and walk. We're talking Lazarus. Where's all the stuff about . . . I don't know . . . her secret life as a stripper. Dressing up in policebint gear as a stripogram . . . Is she kinky about the girls in blue? . . . *I* don't know. *You* tell *me*. You're the one who went on the fishing expedition.'

And in the meantime Veorah, partly (my guess) as a reaction to these developments, has put her life out on the street. Two, perhaps three weeks ago, taking as her starting point the memorial to Yvonne Fletcher in St James's, she set out to walk the route which connects all the London police memorials, travelling alone, responding to whatever turns up, sleeping rough.

Her motives for doing this seem complex and perhaps unknowable, even to herself: she has talked about a sense of compulsion and 'inner necessity' driving her to complete this 'therapeutic itinerary'; of stepping away from the safe and familiar pattern of the everyday in an attempt to find some meaning in the broken pieces of her life; of performing a ritual of cleansing and reclaiming, of *undoing* harm.

She recognised before she started that she was putting herself physically at risk, but believes the potential of harm has to exist if the aim is to live life at a deeper level than it is lived every day; it explains why she has been prepared to give up comfort and safety, accept cold and hunger, and eat whatever comes her way.

After years of feeling she was a sitting target anyway, vulnerable to whatever darkness her husband might choose to bring down on her, she felt strengthened by acting in the world, stepping into the blankness of motorways, loopways and roundabouts, the modern equivalent of the cave or the hermitage in the mountains; walking straight and alone; insignificant, forgotten, metaphorically dead.

This is paraphrasure and, to some extent, supposition. Veorah has a tendency to clam up when you ask her to explain herself head-on. I have been getting it in bits and pieces on tourist postcards (three so far – one of the plump, pink Lady Diana Spencer, one of a punk, one of the spot in the north transept of Canterbury Cathedral where Thomas à Becket was murdered in 1170); also on the backs of menus for tandoori take-aways and bagel boutiques; flyers for failing hairdressers, sandwich bars, tarot readers, minicab firms, the International House of Pancakes, whatever comes to hand. As if the high-toned content of the one side was somehow anchored or counterweighted by the prosaic nature of the information printed on the reverse.

I wasn't able to be there when she kicked off her travels at the Yvonne Fletcher memorial, but I caught up with her four or five days later, when she had got as far as Acton in west London. We had arranged a rendezvous at Wormwood Scrubs – the Scrubs – and when I got there she was standing in front of the security barrier at the main entrance to the prison. She was wearing sweat pants and a hooded top, both the Arctic white – the Arctic *blue*, really – of the soap-powder commercial. It would emerge that she had spent the night before dossing in the cashpoint hall of a Lloyds bank in Hammersmith, but there was no clue to this in her appearance. A sleeping roll was attached to the bottom of her backpack. She was wearing a white baseball cap with her hair pulled through the 'D' above the plastic adjuster and tied in a ponytail.

It was a look – a popular variation was extra-outsize T-shirts that extended to and were knotted at the knee – shared by a number of the women trying to exercise parental control over shoulder-rolling hit squads of grey-faced children and herd them into the visitors' centre. This was a box-shaped temporary building with board walls which were already being drilled from the inside by tiny Nike- and Reebok-shod feet and tiny impatient fists.

'Are you a lifer?' a poster asked. 'Is any member of your family serving a life sentence?' 'Mental illness,' another said. 'What does it mean?' There were posters offering solvent abuse counselling, posters for the Wallasey Wives of Lifers and the Lifers' Support Group; another warning 'Don't let drugs trap you.'

'Chelsea,' a woman bawled as Veorah and I (who were we supposed to be visiting? What were we, nick sniffers?) slunk in. 'Come back over here! What did I tell you, I'll murder you!' Aiming open forehands at the backs of Chelsea's chubby bare legs, Chelsea bent nearly double, so that only one in four slaps connected, arched backwards, skipping forward in a circle, tethered by the hair. Scenes from the dark recesses of urban life, the fly-blown cleats and areas, the blowdown estates, the swarming margins.

A short while earlier an old codger had got on the train a few stops before East Acton and with great concentration started to redistribute cigarettes from a ten-pack of Super-kings into the twenty-packet he was halfway through. He had a prize strawberry hooter, a prison-set sovereign ring knuckle-dusting every finger, and was sporting a rope-banded battered trilby. I remembered when it used to be fives – slim flat packets of five (the corner shops where I lived 'broke' packets and sold the cigarettes as singles) – being transferred to packets of ten. Everybody, for some reason, always took all five cigarettes in one hand at once and then had difficulty (as the old man had had) manoeuvring them into the host packet without mashing them. The tipless white tubes uncoordinated and recalcitrant, prefiguring the joints exploded by arthritis, the knobby arthritic fingers.

Mission eventually accomplished, the old boy shook his wrist a few times, adjusted the expanding metal bracelet, and then put it to his ear to see if he could hear anything. Disappearing gestures, virtually extinct. Blowdown: controlled explosive demolition.

In charge of the visitors' centre was a woman who, even without seeing the gnawed nails and the raised tracks up the inner arms, you'd have had down as a Society girl – a Society beauty, probably; early-fifties vintage, the Princess Margaret set – gone seriously off the rails. She had a lonely pensiveness among the anarchy and chaos; something about the way she batted away the fly that was skidding around the smeary wrapper of a sandwich whose filling was ruled faint against the slices of super-white. She handed us a pair of metal tongs to retrieve the tea bags from the plastic cups of brown-blooming tea.

The only table that was unoccupied was the one nearest the children's corner, something out of a tower block bedroom or women's refuge; a pacifier for the sons and daughters of murderers and stick-up artists, the sprogs of villains.

The main – virtually the only – amenity was a low-walled plastic enclosure bearing the evidence of successive onslaughts of sticky fingers. Covering all of the floor area inside it was a duvet with a Flintstones cartoon cover, and plunked down on this several hand-knitted stuffed toys – a Postman Pat, a brown cat with a pink bow-tie, a Dalmatian-type puppy, a kangaroo and, separated from the kangaroo, eyeless and more or less flattened into two-dimensionality, the baby it once carried tucked into its pouch. The use of dolls as explanatory notes in advance of life-threatening operations. Also as adult-substitutes in cases of sexual abuse of children. 'Just point to where Daddy touched you. Did Daddy touch you there?'

All of them bearing the marks of promiscuous affection. All of them – toys and duvet alike – tending towards the same shade of dishwater grey. Clumps of unwashed fabric. Refugees from Salvation Army bins. A black boombox chained to a radiator pipe. Picture-books and story-books, face-outwards on a shelf: *The Elves and the Shoemaker*; *Marcus the Mole*; *Frog, Duck and Rabbit*; *The Pirate Twins* by William Nicholson; *The Velveteen Rabbit* by Margery Williams.

'Strange to think of hundreds of men locked in cells just a few yards away. Spitting on their hands, flattening their hair, trying to think of things they can talk about, getting themselves up for the visit. Something about them' – I indicated the dirty toys in their dingy enclosure – 'reminds me of them. When you see a dirty toy you think of a fouled child. And so you think of a dysfunctional family. Dirt equals weakness and failure. Perhaps that's why usually when they become torn and dirty, the parents take them and throw them away. They become too real. Exhibits in an autopsy room.'

Veorah had a new scrubbed, no-make-up look which suited her; skin that was reflective and sappy rather than powdered matte. She had unpicked the badge or slogan from the front of her baseball cap, leaving small holes, like the fascia of a store recently gone out of business, through which you could occasionally see the light. Close to her now, I could see that her track suit wasn't as pristine as it had first seemed; it was showing signs of its days on the road and was turning grubby at all the contact points. She said it was her intention to go on wearing it until she had completed the circuit and made it back to the Fletcher memorial in several weeks' time.

'White represents the colour of death in Japan. It establishes the walking pilgrim as an outsider, apart from society. It was either this or a cap of eagle and owl feathers worn with a cape covered with ribbons and stuffed snakes. This seemed more practical.'

The doors of the visitors' centre flew open and a tall black youth stormed in. 'His mum's dyin'. The man's mum's dyin', you know what I'm sayin', an' they won't let me in to tell 'im because my name's not on the VO,' he told the room at large. 'Come in a minicab all the way from Kilburn. Can' *believe* it,' making little impression in the general hubbub, slamming both palms against the wall. A young girl stood up at a nearby table looking improbably tall. She glided past him on medieval-looking roller-blades.

The toe-rags; the twisters; the fucked-up; the fucked-over; the shat-upon; the shitters; the benefit-dependent; the multiply-deprived. The pudding-club brides from the family picture EXCLUSIVES turned into loggy-thighed sofa surfers, one hand on the Malibu, the other on the Maltesers; the remote, the Swans, the Silk Cut neatly stacked. The sailor-suited babies grown into tooled-up scallys, 'mules' for the local front-line dealers – suet-skinned, grainy ghostings of the pictures in the paper (the armed robber who gunned the judge down with his fingers as he was led from the dock; the ferret-face who mimicked tonguing the murdered man's wife as sentence was passed).

'Funny how you can't describe people.' This from a character at the next table. 'Betcha couldn't describe your mum and dad if you were asked. "Take two ashtrays".' The Manhattan skyline razored into the sides and back of his narrow head. Black bars and electronic blotting over the faces.

I asked Veorah if she would get the copy of *The Velveteen Rabbit* that was close to where she was sitting. 'Read me a line,' I said when she had brought it over. 'Any line.'

She looked uncertain. 'A lot of the pages have been torn out.'

'It doesn't matter. Read me something from what's left.'

She flicked backwards and forwards through the pages for a while, still suspecting some trick. Finally she read: ' "Near the house where they lived there was a wood, and in the long June evenings the Boy liked to go there after tea to play." '

' "He took the Velveteen Rabbit with him," ' I picked it up, the text by now being as natural as breathing, ' "and before he wandered off to pick flowers, or play at brigands among the trees, he always made the Rabbit a little nest somewhere among the bracken, where he would be quite cosy, for he was a kind-hearted little boy and he liked Bunny to be comfortable." '

I saw her nipples stiffen against the snowy track suit top. 'Try me on another bit,' I said.

' "And so the little Rabbit was put into a sack with the old picture-books and a lot of rubbish, and carried out to the end of the garden behind the old fowl-house." '

' "That was a fine place to make a bonfire, only the gardener was too busy just then to attend to it. He had the potatoes to dig and the green peas to gather, but next morning he promised to come quite early and burn the whole lot." '

'Learned at Nanny's knee?' Veorah said. 'Still pining for the banked fire and tea in the nursery. I bet you still take your old teddy bear to bed.'

It was time for the visits to begin. Semi-surreptitious arrangements were underway, gobbets of cling-wrapped heroin and ganja being made available for easy mouth-to-mouth transferral, and then concealment in the lifer's already greased or Nivea'd jacksie.

In one of the streets behind the prison, an ice-cream van's chimes played the Harry Lime theme.

Braybrook Street, site of the fourth memorial on her itinerary, was a five-minute walk from the Scrubs. The back of the prison, its surveillance towers, the continuous concrete goitre that is a recent addition to the perimeter wall, was seventy yards from the carved rose marble. It was unwittingly arriving at the scene of a planned break-out that cost the three policemen their lives – they were gunned down on the edge of the piece of common land that was being lightly drizzled on when Veorah and I shuffled up. She walked around the memorial appraisingly for a minute or so, and then quietly set about doing what she had to do.

In addition to being pink, it differed from the others in being a more or less conventional headstone shape – as if three of the ball-and-stalk memorials had been brought together, the tallest in the middle, the spaces between them smoothed away.

Although it has only recently been erected, it gave the date of the shootings as August 12, 1966. The World Cup summer. Bobby Moore. Mooro. 1941–1993. Who now has a memorial of his own. Death and the cult of dead figures. The 'very special dead'.

Braybrook Street is a crescent of red-brick, pre-War council semis. For a brief stretch near the prison the houses stare across the street at each other. Mostly though – and this is true of the houses opposite the memorial – the prospect is of the common, and then the wilder Scrubs, still with some signs of the marsh trails existing there before London was built, and then the round-the-clock UFO spotlights of what could be a container terminal or industrial park.

Laid on for the curtain-twitchers that afternoon though – and there were a couple, plus a couple of elderly locals with shoppers on wheels, spectating from a distance – was a piece of living theatre which might have had them rushing to the phone to report an act of blood sacrifice or black satanic ritual.

Veorah had laid a trail of yellow seeds in a wide circle around the memorial. Now she was in the circle, moving slowly around it, performing various rites involving a lighted candle and a ball of teased-out cotton wool. The ground was muddy and sparsely covered but she dropped to her knees and said what sounded like (she was speaking softly): 'I am here at last. I am glad to be here.' After a further few minutes she touched the flame of the candle to the cotton wool which shrivelled instantly to a cinder. The warm rain that was still falling quickly extinguished the slugs of wriggling red flame.

She dispersed the seeds with her foot, then, reaching into her pack for a small camera, clicked off a couple of snaps. These would end up in the journal she was keeping of her journey which even then, just a few days in, already contained many texts, and pictures of the ragpickers, box dwellers, runaways and the assorted loony tunes she had encountered along the way.

She had produced this back at the visitors' centre, obviously intending to regale me with her traveller's tales, her on-the-road stories, until I made it clear that my ears were closed. 'There are twenty thousand stories under the sky and I've heard too many of them from the horse's mouth. I am not involved.'

'What goes on in the sea is of no interest to the rock,' she said. She said that, in the Japanese tradition, she planned to have the texts and pictures – pictures of strangers, photographed for the last, perhaps the only time, in their lives; destitutes, indigents – put in her coffin when she was dead.

wabi – the concept of poverty; exterior poor, interior rich; *angya* – ascetic training through travelling or pilgrimage; *settai* – the custom of giving succour to pilgrims; *chin-kon* – pacification and deepening of the soul

'The walking ascetic pilgrim remains an outsider, apart from society. Dressing in pilgrim's clothes and walking the route amidst the symbols of modernity actually intensify the sense of separation between the pilgrim and the mundane world, and the sense of being dead to the world'

'The omnipresent images of death that permeate
the pilgrimage, and that are found in the pilgrim's clothing'

'An underlying assumption of pilgrimage has always been
that by covering ground physically, one also progresses
spiritually'

'Kneel on wet stones, walk barefoot over sharp scree,
wade through icy water . . . The raw experience of
hunger, cold, lack of sleep . . . Fasting, sleeplessness,
suffering and endurance'

'Pilgrims might climb thousands of feet, sleep in plain
board guesthouses, eat rice gruel and a few pickles, and
circumambulate set routes burning incense and bowing
at site after site'

'It is through an analysis of space that we grasp what the
course we set through the world of the near by has in
common with courses through the world of the far away'

'Traces of a vast network of well-marked trails are still
found throughout the land. They were trampled down
by musicians, monks, merchants, porters, pilgrims and
periodic armies'

'Though I can plan to make a pilgrimage, which is a rite
projected in space, I cannot plan for what the pilgrimage
will make of me'

'Embracing the solitude of squares, the desolation of the
streets, the devastation of the buildings'

The street people (Veorah's new friends) have this in
common with the street shrines that materialise overnight
on train platforms and suburban street corners and busy
city intersections: both used to be regarded as something
temporary and aberrant; both are now regarded as semi-
permanent, semi-official additions to urban life.

Fifteen minutes ago, I passed bunches of flowers, both faded and fresh, and soft toys tied with ribbons to every reachable part of the vast trunk of a tree close to where a group of children were recently mowed down by a lorry.

Four or five streets further on was a shrine erected in memory of an Asian shopkeeper who was murdered when he refused to hand over the takings of his till. The flowers and plants that were originally laid have been replaced by more permanent materials – breeze block, bitumen, a metal grille over the shallow alcove where a garlanded Hindu deity has been installed. The simple hut structure is surmounted by a pineapple cupola, pointed in lapis, leafed in gold.

After this, the police memorial to Alan King, stabbed four years ago on this busy road in the netherness of E17, can only look impoverished, insignificant. The scar that once disfigured it has been repaired. But the memorial has been kept low – it stands probably no higher than two feet – to conform with the height of the stone wall against which it has been erected. This would make it invisible, for example, to the occupants of the small block of flats in front of which the stabbing took place, which was perhaps the thinking of those responsible for its siting.

Not that these were my first thoughts as I reached the point on Higham Hill Road to clock in with Veorah re her suggestion in her letter. My first thought was how two weeks, perhaps a little longer, could have brought about such a seismic change in her appearance. Perched on the wall, swinging her legs, fitting her camera away among her belongings was Madame Blavatsky, a post-apocalyptic Tina Turner, a Masai warrior wife.

She looked like a poster of the person who had started out, bespattered by traffic and defaced by idling schoolboys at a bus stop. I had had an image of her on her travels, pressing on through the grain of the city, slicked by the lights of cars and emphatic coloured signs. In the image, these washed over her, leaving no trace. Now it was as if every light that had touched her had penetrated the fabric of her clothes and become fixed as a stain.

At some point she had reversed the sweat pants and track suit top and was now wearing the fleecy side out. This had increased the absorbency and potential for garnering dirt, which was distributed about her person in jammy, eggy clumps. The baseball cap wasn't *as* filthy, but it was smudged and stained. Beneath it, her face looked like a mis-registered picture reproduced on the lowest-grade newsprint – eyes in the cheekbones, mouth in the neck. This was the effect produced by the stripes of fluorescent sun block – orange, pink, chalk white, magenta – with which she had let rip. She seemed radiant, eyes and teeth gleaming through the mask.

We are drinking sweet milky drinks in a Walthamstow greasy spoon aspiring to franchise status with pictures of beefburgers and plates of spaghetti on wipeable display folders, and I ask the usual question: Where did you sleep last night? 'In the doorway of a branch of Kookaï not far from here with a boy who has had an incredible life. His grandmother was a singer with the Bavarian State Opera, and . . . ' Steam hisses out of a copper boiler, forming clouds around the litho-on-canvas picture of a harbourside village in Larnaka with the swans and the Vespas under the trees and the old men playing checkers at the unshaded tables outside the bar . . . Cigarette smoke curling between our faces.

Veorah rummages in her pack and passes me a letter she

says was left for her at the memorial in Knightsbridge by the mother of one of the victims of the Harrods bombing. 'The weather reflected the anger of Mother Nature,' it reads in part, 'a howling fitful mournful wind blew, and the atmosphere was loaded with sorrow and anguish. Dismal squalls of rain fell. (A pall of smoke rose hundreds of feet high.) Crowds fled down Knightsbridge, Sloane Street, Brompton Road, and up to Hyde Park Corner.

'May you be blest. Her Mother'.

And then a postscript: 'As if it were yesterday'

'Of all the things I've seen,' the Noh mask says, 'the thing I think I will be haunted by are men's shirts hanging in bedroom windows. Always white. White shirts on wire hangers hanging up to dry. At nights a bare lightbulb glowing through them. I've got dozens of pictures. Early on, I started to take a picture of every one I saw.'

When she goes home to Seaton, her last act will be a ritual incineration of her once-white suit.

She has been offered a place to sleep for the night by a local allotment holder. The allotments are adjacent to the block of flats where the memorial stands. 'Trencherfield Fertility Association', a board at the gate announces. 'Allotments. Trading Shed. Vacant Plots.' Hemmed in by housing on three sides, the road on the fourth; a slash-and-burn clearing, an unexpected village in the forest, an anomalous open tract.

We crunch along the cinder path between bean frames, plastic cloches, leeks and sprouts triumphing over the Iron Age mud, the acid soil. Men hoeing, leaning on spades, exchanging banter with a neighbour on the next plot; women in aluminium folding chairs, knitting, repositioning themselves away from the shadows, disappearing into the dusk.

Veorah's pensioner waits by his hen run. A man in a bib-overall, tweed jacket, odd laces in his boots. There is a water butt, a creosoted out-house, green tomatoes set out on a window ledge to grow ripe. But the heart of the operation is a pigeon loft with plank steps and a raised wooden platform at the front, and a white-and-yellow picket fence traversing the roof. The birds are individually caged behind bars of wood dowelling, and their names inked onto cards. Many of these seem to be in Dutch (Prins, Kadet, Genopte, Donker), but some are in English: 'Bright Star', 'Super Star', 'Shining Star', 'Shooting Star', 'Milky Way', 'Killer King'.

The old man removes the bird called Super Star from its cage and expertly upends it, its feet trapped between two of his middle fingers, the quartzite feathers around its neck showing to advantage. 'A good bird for a dirty day,' he says, a man anxious not to get too much into his stride, warned many times by his wife in the past of the danger of boring non-fanciers into the ground.

Veorah had met him earlier, when she had presumably given an explanation for her appearance. Now, showing the pigeon is his way of introducing himself to me. 'My beauty,' he coos to the bird, flexing one wing and then the other; smoothing a finger over its gently pulsing breast. 'See the difference between this one and a street rat,' he says, indicating the legs and feet, which he says he cleans with a mixture of lemon juice and baby oil. The architecture of the bones seems to glow through the skin, which is violet and trans-lucent.

The ring is loose on its leg and reminds me for some reason of the rings sealing off the flesh of Heath Hawkins's

talismanic small hands – a thought that is immediately extinguished when I notice the late strawberries, the old man's gift
to Veorah, stacked in a cardboard nesting-bowl on a bin of
grain.

At Wormwood Scrubs, Veorah had been invited to spend
the night in the visitors' centre: she had stepped into the
low-walled plastic enclosure when everyone had gone and
settled herself down on the dingy duvet among the cheap
soiled toys.

Now she is soiled, symbolically stained by the bad karma
and rogue energies she has been clearing up along the route.
Filthy and fleecy like a toy that has been twisted, turned,
scratched, shaken, banged against the wall, thrown to the
ground (the disturbing pleasures of involuntary cruelty and
humiliation); on all fours, laying out a sleeping bag on the
sawdust floor of the murmuring pigeon coop.

E:I:G:H:T

I would like to switch off, but my mind keeps scratching away, working up an intro. 'The police helicopter with its flickering and sweeping, thirty-million-candlepower lights is raking the streets like a stream of urgent piss being played against a urinal.'

Fancy. Fanciful, even. Okay. (And of course I wouldn't get away with 'piss'.) But I think I am allowed this. It is late. I have been drinking. I spent the ten hours before I started drinking fielding abuse on crapulous, scrapheap estates, braving killer dogs, hanging on the knocker. Now it's R and R time in the 'Trident' bar of the hotel, and the bottles pop and the bar tabs slide into treble figures as we all try to shit each other that *we* have bought up the Devil Girls' mothers/brothers/poxy junkie lovers.

The Devil Girls. Correction: **DEVIL GIRLS** The Devil Girls – and the drinks are on them – are Hayley Bonelli and Maria Scalabrino, aged fifteen and sixteen. Italian, obviously. Originally. Third- or fourth-generation English-Italian and part of a small, long-established Italian community here.

Although it already feels like weeks, it is only three nights since Hayley and Maria earned their tabloid moniker by murdering the neighbour's children they were supposed to be taking care of. Off their faces on acid, speed and estate-bottled rough cider, they took, Mitsubishi Diamante, aged six weeks, and Sudio Porsche Carrera, aged twenty months, by their left legs and beat them against the wall. The indentations made by their heads were discovered by the babies' mother when she returned home soon after midnight.

This happened on the fifteenth floor of a tower block called Ullswater House. (All the blocks were – unfacetiously – named after beauty spots in the Lakeland arcadia just a few miles to the north.) The Bonellis and Scalabrinos, the devil girls' families, live on different floors of the same building. *Lived.* As word spread through the estate about what had happened, vigilante groups spontaneously combusted. Italian shops were torched; people with Italian names, or known Italian connections, were driven from their homes. Cars were dragged into the middle of the street and burned, and riot police battered by bricks and petrol bombs. Street lamps were felled with sledgehammers, plunging most of the estate into darkness. Then the electricity substation was burned out after petrol was poured over its circuits.

Shortly before dawn, the whereabouts of Tony Bonelli, Hayley's father, were discovered. He had been given refuge in another flat in Ullswater House and, when he realised the mob were on to him, fled to the roof of his building. Cornered by youths equipped with screwdrivers and pickhandles, he scrambled onto the parapet and dived to his death.

Since then, the looting, torching and running battles between police and rioters have continued. They're going on out there somewhere now. The occasional flare turns phosphorescent as it meets the thirty-million-candlepower police beam. The sky flushes briefly red, followed by a mini-mushroom cloud that signals another Astra or Nova or police

222

Ford Cosworth going up. A local stringer for the *Star* has drawn the short straw and been nominated our man on the spot, running back hot-foot with the details should anything go off.

Meanwhile we sit here getting crocked and giving it that about who we've pulled, got alongside, bought up, boxed off. Money talk. Trade gossip.

'. . . Now he is an A-1 example of somebody failing up'
'. . . He's only started to fuckin' refer to the rag as *Qualipop*'
'. . . There are only three big Gets out there at the minute – Di, Whacko Jacko and Lucan'
'. . . Can I check I've got what the plod said'
'. . . Everything's a one-shot deal. You get it or you don't'
'. . . "Ethics" is his classic. "That's that place to the east of London where they all wear white socks" '
'. . . Through the wall he hears him say to her, "Here's five shillings. Go an' buy yourself a new hut" '
'. . . All the fiddles in the warehouse, the machine room, the process department'.

Heath Hawkins upsets a hackette who thinks nobody knows she had a bunk-up with him the night before last by producing the picture of a child mauled by a Rottweiler. 'Have you ever thought about counselling? I think you're sick.'

'What would you know about *sick*. If you want sick, I'll show you sick, you smelly shitbag fucking bastard bitch.'

Two older hacks are competing with each other doing one-arm push-ups on the floor.

'I was told in all seriousness by a sniper in Sarajevo, "I am happy to kill a child when he is with his mother, because there is something fantastic on the face of the mother." They only pussied out of using it.'

'One night in a forest I saw a Khmer Rouge hoist the smallest boy in a family by his ankles and in front of his family this was swing him so that his head struck the trunk of a palm tree.'

A non-resident asks if he can pay his bill with plastic. 'These days we take anything. I'd accept a note from your mother.'

'There's only one job advertised on the noticeboard at the Job Centre in town here – "Security work. Furness area. One pound fifty an hour. Bring your own dog." '

'Did you get the stuff about the Bonelli guy, the father, having his ears pierced a few years ago by a friend with an ice cube and a carpet tack?'

Tuning out and in.

'. . . One thing you can say about Carson. If bullshit was music, he'd be a brass band.'

'. . . buying in spiders to keep the greenfly and blackfly down in the atrium.'

Still framing and re-framing the intro. I don't know why. As far as intros go, I am surplus to requirements. Curtis Preece's demise has cleared the way for Sebastian-Dominic to move up the pecking order; and he has brought in his own new young hotshot news features scribe. I'm here in the role of legman, errand-runner, fatter of his puny paragraphs.

The police helicopter strobes our faces as it clatters over the hotel. 'We got ten minutes to get the last fuckin' chopper out of here, man,' Heath says.

The bar staff in their grease-rimmed, ill-fitting shirts, waiting to go home.

What is odd – what is *really* odd, and making me raw to the endless disparaging comments about the things people say and do oop here, broad take-offs of the accent – is that this used to be my town. That is, I grew up here, came back on regular, although increasingly infrequent visits during the time when my parents were still alive, remember when the hotel where we are staying was built and the buildings that were cleared to make way for it – the mussels and whelks shop, the wool shop where my mother started work at thirteen, the rag shop where I took rags to be sorted and weighed, the reeking piles, the crepuscular scales, the light streaming through knot-holes in the wooden structure. Behind the rag shop, the stables where the rag-and-bone-men bedded down their ponies, the ponies in their old brass-inlay leather blinkers, dragged steaming up the wooden ramp. In many ways, it was like a country town, with a town-centre slaughter yard, livestock market, feed store, hills visible at the ends of the terraced streets, the cranes from the shipyard poking into the sky.

What is even odder – and so far it is something I have managed to keep to myself – is that Brigg flats, as the estate that is currently drawing all the heat is known, is the estate where we used to live. More: Ullswater House was the last place here that I thought of as home. It was from Ullswater House that I set out to start the newspapering job in the Midlands which was to launch me on my amazing career.

We stayed on a waiting list for a number of years, accumu-lating the points we needed to qualify for a place in one of the new multi-storeys, gazing longingly skywards from our fungal back-to-back at the stellar windows of Ullswater and Derwentwater and Coniston House.

In her job as a cleaner my mother somehow came into possession of some discarded blueprint linen from the offices of the architects who designed Brigg flats. This was washed out and used as a table cloth when she laid a table on Sundays. Traces of the drawing were still clearly visible – kitchen stacked above kitchen, bathroom above bathroom, the strict regularity making the services cheaper to install – and the three of us sat gazing into the faded plans and elevations, at the walls – the 'commonplace good dullness' – we hoped one day would contain us.

In the early eighties, Ullswater House, which had stood for nearly thirty years by then, was retrofitted and recladded, the roughcast concrete blocks of the original overlaid with an uninflected synthetic cream skin. By that point the 'decent' families had started to move out to estates on the periphery, and the crack addicts, muggers and ram-raiders had started to move in. Flats were stripped, copper cable ripped out, radiators sold for scrap, entire floors burned out and boarded up. The tenants who remain protect their territory with big dogs tethered to the balconies. Filled nappies rain down from the upper storeys. Another hazard for pedestrians is the number of people throwing themselves off the roofs. (In the week before Tony Bonelli, a man leapt from Coniston House clutching two carrier bags of supermarket shopping.)

The Prince Monolulu – the 'Mong' – used to be a quiet local, the haunt of old men studying the horses, rolling their own, and playing dominoes and cards. Now it is where the loansharks and estate 'enforcers' hang out: members of local firms following police movements on scanners, doing speed-balls, injecting cider into their veins, watching tapes of them-selves 'roguing' and 'displaying', laying rubber, doing hand-brake turns and wheelies in front of the impotent Bill in stolen Renault turbos and Golf GTIs. The bandits flash and chirrup inside padlocked, wrought-iron, baseball-bat-proof cages with minimal holes for the hands.

You don't just walk into the Mong. You have to be invited. And Heath had arranged a meet with some of the top men who had already taken care of his drugging needs and said they could get us into the flat where Mitsubishi Diamante and Sudio Porsche Carrera were murdered, which they did.

Forensics had completed their business; Linda Bundy, the mother, had been absented, and they seemed to have the run of the place. It was clean, modestly furnished, with a painted mask from Japan, some miniature statues of Romans with heads and limbs lopped off, a goldfish swimming in just enough water to support life, trailing a thready discharge, round and round a miniature castle, the rings of evaporation sedimented around the bowl.

There was the line of the sofa (had they moved it to give themselves a bigger target area?) and, below it, the two clean bloodless head shapes imbedded in the wall. Heath got me to place my fist inside each of them in turn to show the scale. This reminded me of the survivor of an attack by a serial killer who encouraged me to put my fist in the deep depression which, although new hair had grown over it, still cratered her skull.

There were syringes rolling around the lift in which my mother had had to be brought down vertically in her coffin. There was a strap of nylon webbing across her forehead holding her in place, like the internal straps of the suitcases she used to pack when we were going off on caravan holidays when I was young.

Later that night they came for Heath at the hotel and held a knife at his throat until he had drawn up to his limit at the nearest money machine.

Most of the warehouses on the docks have been turned into restaurants and bars. And many of these come under the control in one way or another of Frank Leppard. 'As of this minute I am worth one million, one hundred and sixty four thousand, four hundred and seventy three pounds and twenty-eight pence,' was the first thing he said to me tonight, although I hadn't seen him for a dozen years. 'And I'm accountable to nobody. I could spend it tomorrow. It's all mine. Oh! The money's horrendous.'

I was at school with Frank. He went from school into the shipyards, following his father. The last time I saw him he was doing unisex hairdressing and repro pub mirrors. 'Fat bastard,' he said. 'I'm a fat bastard. We've both turned into fat bastards.'

We took a tour of his principality. This meant following him through dustbin areas and cellars and dark, hot-walled passages so that he might appear as if by magic at the heart of the action and surprise somebody with their hand in the till or handing out a dirty glass or violating any of the many staff protocols he has established. (Lipstick must be red or crimson, this does not mean orange. Waitresses must not wear black bras under white shirts. Male bar staff will limit themselves to *one* ear-ring.)

From Blinkers to Quavers to Boobs to Bangles to Berlins. A swift schooner here, a demi-carafe there. Here a hit, there a quaff. A curry pizza.

Tonight I have learned (in so far as I'm capable of remembering what I've learned) two things. People drink 'prestige' lagers straight from the bottle because if you pour it into a glass nobody knows you've paid £1.85 for your drink. (In places like the Mong there is the added consideration that draught beer is easier to spike with substances that render you incapable of offering any resistance when they eventually roll you.) Two: it costs Frankie twelve hundred pounds a week in replacement glassware. (This was as close as either of us came to any form of personal disclosure.)

Being at the Brother at least meant I could allow him to drop me off where I am staying. It's not the best place to be, but it isn't scraping the barrel either, although they tried. (Did they try.) In fact I fell lucky. I have ended up being allocated an Executive-King at the standard Single rate.

My key was missing from Reception, which has alerted me to the possibility of Hawkins pulling a stunt he has pulled more than once in the past – running up a lot of room service from my room, on my account. And, sure enough, as I round the corner, I can see that parked in the corridor outside room 319 is a service trolley with all flaps raised to accommodate the detritus of what seems to have been a Lucullan tuck-in – domed platters, gravied plates, bread rolls still swaddled in their linen nappy, soiled napkins, lightly perspiring cheese. And bottles. More bottles than even Hawkins could have got through on his own.

'Who is it?' In response to my rap on the door.

'Who do you think it is, Father Christmas? Who were you expecting?'

On the bed is a woman who I have never met but recognise instantly. I also recognise the hands – the clawy fingers of the hands from the black draw-string bag Hawkins wears around his neck.

The woman on the bed is Patsy Bonelli, mother of Hayley devil girl. She is naked, her legs pulled wide apart, her feet somehow tethered. Kneeling on the bed beside her, also naked, is Robin Carson. The two small hands have been pushed up in the space between the woman's legs, tarantulous fingers against the lilac-white thighs: a trapped creature tearing an exit, a body leaving her body.

There has been a hole opening up in the seam behind the little dog's head, and Carson has used this to skewer it on his erection.

Hawkins steps from behind the door and crashes a light in my face.

So this is me. Caught. Snatched. Definitively captured. KIA. Killed in action. TSD. Time since death. The nineteenth-century conviction that the last thing seen at the point of death would be fixed, as in a photograph, on the surface of the eye.

'Sucking on the devil's dick,' Hawkins says. He is speeding, grinding his molars; his jaws really grinding. 'We're dancing with the devil, Norman. We're doing the cha-cha-cha. We're doing the slow drag.'

It is the early hours, but there are people about in the streets, just walking. Parents with children; young people in uniform hooded tops playing tapes of motorway traffic, glass smashing, family quarrels at full volume on the boxes toted on their shoulders.

People straggling out of side streets, falling in, merging; a low-budget Wartime musical; the march up to the mill-owner's house, the deposition to the pit boss's mansion. 'Crowds of people moved through the streets with a dream-like violence.' My feet taking me past shops disappeared behind roller shutters, the interiors cut up into volumes of chain-link fencing, to the only place they know with any certainty they have been before.

The lift lobby at Ullswater House is a dungeon of shattered glass and compacted litter. 'Rat-piss hell' sprayed in metal paint. It is here, on a small patch of dirt and grass, that they have erected the shrine.

For a skeleton they have taken a cage from one of the pub machines and walled it in with empty cans of High Strength Lager. The canopy has been constructed from strips of orange police caution tape worked into a stole or alb. Items of the children's clothing have been laid inside – small T-shirts, thick-washed white and pink synthetics – along with some of their toys: a pink elephant, a tiger, a green horse. Night-lights float in a tank, surrounded by picture candles. Yellow ribbons, hardly yellow any more, years after the release of the last hostage, have been stripped from car aerials and fastened to the frame. A cable-lead from a third- or fourth-storey window supplies the power to the television playing home-video footage of Mitsubishi Diamante and Sudio Porsche Carrera from pre-birth – streaky black-and-white pre-natal scans – to almost the day of their deaths. Shaky zoom-ins on drooly smiling faces, a hand reaching for a tinselly Christmas tree, the first child being joined by her new sister. The linking backdrop is the yellow-gold medallion-patterned wallpaper of the room where they were murdered, the ornamental limbless figures, the goldfish in its bowl.

Out of the darkness a steady stream of figures coming forward, waiting to kiss the spar of the cage that one of Heath's assailants repeatedly cleans with a rag of silk.

Out of the darkness a steady stream of figures coming forward, waiting to kiss the spar of the cage that one of Heath's assailants repeatedly cleans with a rag of silk.

The spectre, hanging back, recording. Re-formatting, word-counting, re-nosing experience; putting a headline on it before it has a chance to be felt. Telling it in words that will never see black and white.